In this excellent book Davi erable
gifts as a first-rate mathema ssible
manner. The result is not ng: its
insights have the potentia of the
Church in its efforts to mak hope it
will be very widely read.

Dr John Inge, Bishop of Worcester

God's Belongers is an accessible book crafted by a research scientist. It is accessible because Bishop David is a master of his field. Working within the discipline of empirical theology, Bishop David has developed and tested his theories through rigorous surveys and stringent statistical analyses. His evidence challenges the Church to think differently about aspects of ministry and mission that really matter. A strong doctrine of creation leads to a theology of individual differences that respects human diversity. An inclusive ecclesiology rejoices in multiple ways of belonging to God's Church. A grasp of religious orientation theory acknowledges and respects multiple pathways to discipleship. Here is an accessible book which, taken seriously, could change the way in which we think of God and, consequently, think of God's Church. Now this really is theology in action.

Revd Canon Professor Leslie J. Francis, Warwick University

This book provides a really helpful tool for parishes and cathedrals who are seeking to reach out to and engage with those who might be described as 'occasional churchgoers'. It offers insights into the many ways in which people engage with the Church at different levels. Statistics suggest that Christian faith is alive and well amongst many who choose to attend church less frequently and that they have something important to teach the Church about the diverse ways in which Christian faith and mission is lived out and expressed in our world today. David Walker suggests ways in which the Church might encourage and support them as much as its regular attenders.

The Venerable Cherry Vann, Archdeacon of Rochdale

The Bible Reading Fellowship
15 The Chambers, Vineyard
Abingdon OX14 3FE
brf.org.uk

The Bible Reading Fellowship (BRF) is a Registered Charity (233280)

ISBN 978 0 85746 467 5
First published 2017
10 9 8 7 6 5 4 3 2 1 0
All rights reserved

Text © David Walker 2017
The author asserts the moral right to be identified as the author of this work

Cover images © Thinkstock, Lesley Cox, Luke Roberts and Ian Leadbetter

Acknowledgements
Unless otherwise stated, scripture quotations are taken from The Holy Bible, New International
Version (Anglicised edition) copyright © 1979, 1984, 2011 by Biblica. Used by permission of
Hodder & Stoughton Publishers, an Hachette UK company. All rights reserved. 'NIV' is a registered
trademark of Biblica. UK trademark number 1448790.

Every effort has been made to trace and contact copyright owners for material used in this
resource. We apologise for any inadvertent omissions or errors, and would ask those concerned
to contact us so that full acknowledgement can be made in the future.

A catalogue record for this book is available from the British Library

Printed and bound by CPI Group (UK) Ltd, Croydon CR0 4YY

God's Belongers

How people engage with God today and how the church can help

David Walker

For Leo, whose journey has just begun.

Contents

Part 3: Who else is missing?

Foreword

Whenever the church gets to talking about numbers, sooner or later someone will protest that it is not all about bums on seats, is it? Well, yes and no. As this readable and insightful book from David Walker makes clear, belonging cannot simply be measured by your attendance record. There are multiple ways of belonging to any organisation or community, and especially the church. But if instead of 'bums on seats' the church talked about 'hearts being changed' or 'lives being transformed', and once we realise that there can be no impact in our local communities and wider society unless there are at least some people who not only belong, but whose belonging shapes and directs the whole of their lives, i.e. their hearts are being changed and their lives are being transformed, then we begin to see that understanding how people belong and ministering to people in their different ways of belonging is something worth thinking about. This book will help you.

The Rt Revd Stephen Cottrell
Bishop of Chelsford

Introduction:
an aid for mission

What's this book about?

I'm the twelfth person to hold the title of Bishop of Manchester since the diocese was created in 1847. Only one of us, William Temple, has gone on to greater things, first as Archbishop of York and then, all too briefly, to Canterbury. It was Temple who coined the statement that the Church is the only institution ever to be created for the benefit of those who are not its members. It's a wonderfully succinct phrase. It captures the notions of both our pastoral and evangelistic ministry to the communities and nations within which we, the Church, have been set. It brings with it a strong whiff that we are indeed a 'priestly people', called for the good of others. True to his own vision, Temple was co-founder of the post-World War II Welfare State.

If Temple had the great vision, then it was around 40 years after his death that the worldwide Anglican Communion put the next level of detail into it, through the promulgation of the *Five Marks of Mission*. This balanced agenda of evangelism, nurture, care for the needy, concern for the environment and challenge to injustice has won wide respect and support from around the world. It continues to provide a checklist, lest the Church be tempted to reduce the scope of its mission to some smaller, narrower, more congenial subset. But it recognises that the way in which mission is embodied, in vastly different societies and cultures, will vary.

This book is my personal attempt to grapple with Temple's vision. It's founded in the simple premise that if we want to be the Church for those who are not our members, then the first thing we have to do is to get to know them. God so loved the world that he sent his Son, Jesus, to live among us. It isn't just an accident of history, the lack of the modern mechanisms of communicating remotely, that meant that most of what he did, he did face to face. Jesus listened to people, absorbed their stories and then responded. The stories that he told show how acutely he was observing the society around him, everything from the natural phenomena of the weather through to the overt and hidden motivations that underlie human actions.

For us to claim to be continuing Christ's mission, yet to bypass the effort to understand the people and society around us, seems to me to be a contradiction in terms. And yet it's a trap that churches all too often fall into. We take our mission directly from our theology, or from what somebody tells us we ought to be doing, or from what is most congenial and least threatening to our own preferences. Bishops can be just as guilty as anyone else at trying to impose mission priorities and initiatives across the hugely diverse territory of our dioceses as though they had been handed down on tablets of stone. We need to be humble enough to take the time to observe, and observe carefully, the people and places around us. Much of what is written here is my own attempt to do just that. It draws on 17 years of parish ministry and another 15 as bishop. Many of the examples of mission that I give are taken directly from my own experience. To that extent, this is the sort of book that many reflective Christian ministers could write, and indeed many do. The way I've done that reflection, however, is very much rooted in my own personal story. And for that I need to tell you a little about my earlier background.

In the autumn of 1979, as a young graduate student who had just begun a doctorate in Pure Mathematics, I went to see the dean of my college chapel to explain that I had a problem. For some time I'd been aware of a growing sense of vocation to ordained ministry. I'd tried to do a deal with God, whereby I would continue in research until I reached the age of 30, after which I'd happily go into pastoral ministry. But God wouldn't shake hands on it. The call had become increasingly urgent. I needed to offer myself for ordination now. I can't remember a great deal of what the dean said to me, except for one thing. He assured me that, though I might be giving up mathematics for now, God would find some way of using my abilities and aptitudes at some point in the future. By the following autumn I was at Queen's Theological College in Birmingham.

For the next quarter of a century my mathematical abilities went on the back burner. And then, almost by chance, I discovered, right at the point when I was about to undertake my first-ever clergy sabbatical, a group of theologians who had a use for numbers. Empirical Theology takes as its particular focus the understanding of how people, in many cases ordinary Christians or members of wider society, live out their lives. It examines their beliefs, attitudes and behaviours. It listens, with the same care and attention with which Jesus himself listened, to what people have to say about themselves and about God. A lot of its work is through interviewing individuals and building up a picture from case studies. But some of it involves numbers, more precisely, statistics. Its sister fields of research are those of the Sociology and Psychology of Religion. Empirical Theology adds to what study in those fields can achieve by providing an overt theological as well as a general academic analysis of what is being observed.

The two things that mathematicians play with are most simply summarised as patterns and numbers. What you will find in this book are the patterns that emerged when I began to conduct statistical surveys among groups of people who turned up in churches on special occasions, along with a few of the most important numbers. Underlying what I've written is, at times, some quite sophisticated statistical analysis. If you are minded to try to understand that stuff, then there are a whole series of academic papers in which I set out and published my findings, so that they could be scrutinised by the best academic minds in the field. You'll find a list of some of them at the back of this book. But for the sake of the vast majority of readers, many of whom will have given up maths with some relief in their mid-teens, you won't find much by way of statistical argument or proof here in this present text.

The figures I use for most of my statistics come from two surveys that I carried out. The first, in the autumn of 2007, was a study of around 1450 people who turned up at rural Harvest services in my then diocese of Worcester. It was a remarkable response rate and I'm extremely grateful to the clergy and lay leaders in the 27 parishes that took part for allowing my questionnaire to be completed in their churches, usually before or after the service. I was able to ask questions about why people had come to the service, what they believed about the Christian faith, their attitudes to various public issues, and their relationships with other Christians in their community, as well as how often they came to church, read the Bible and said their prayers.

The second survey took place in Worcester, at the two main cathedral carol services in the immediate run up to Christmas 2009. A slightly shorter version of it was then repeated at Lichfield Cathedral the following year. Once again, I need to express my thanks to their respective deans, chapters and volunteers, especially the sidesmen and women who handed out and collected in hundreds of survey forms, right in the middle of their busiest time of year. The phenomenon of going to church at Christmas has long fascinated me, and this study allowed me to put a whole range of questions to a group of people, almost half of whom admitted to coming to church no more than a handful of times a year. Why were they there? What did they make of the Christmas story? What degree of previous or present church background did they have? What were their views on some topical religious issues?

In addition, the Worcester survey added two final sections which were based on important areas within Empirical Theology, Psychological Type and Religious Orientation. But more of that later.

As well as to mathematics, this book owes a great deal to the concept of a 'Theology of Individual Differences'. At its simplest this begins with the precept that God has made each of us, each in his own image, and yet each of us different and unique. If he had wanted to make us all the same, that option was available. Individual difference exists, not in order that some should be saved and others condemned, as some of the reformer John Calvin's disciples have argued, but because it is part of the richness of creation.

The call of God is a universal call. It is to be issued to all, and in the form they will best be able to hear and respond to. If what we observe is that some groups in our society, who should be equally able to hear the call, appear to be responding to different extents, then that ought to be a cause of concern. And indeed, where it is observable, it often is. We rightly worry when church congregations seem to contain far too few men, or younger adults, or those living with disabilities or people from different ethnic backgrounds. But that is because such differences are often highly visible. What about the other, invisible but equally important, differences that might be reflected in lower numbers of certain types of people appearing to respond to God's call? Should it not equally be a cause for concern if our churches were almost exclusively populated by, for example, extraverts? Would that not suggest that we had got something just as wrong in the ways we are articulating God's call as if almost all churchgoers were male?

The first section of this book sets out one particular way in which I have found people differ, namely in the ways in which they experience and enact belonging. In the first chapter I will set out a model in which I describe how people belong to God and to the church in four distinct ways: through people, places, one-off events and regular activities. The next four chapters then go on to look at each of these dimensions in turn. Each of them is informed by the two surveys that I carried out as part of my research, and I've given a few examples of that in the text. This model of belonging does, however, pose a challenge to some traditional ways of thinking about Church and mission.

This challenge lies in the fact that only one of the four dimensions of belonging has a direct relationship with coming frequently to church. There's a lot of evidence from other studies that there are people who have ceased to be a part of a regular church congregation, other than by way of incapacity, and yet who retain in all other aspects, and not just for a period of time, strong evidence of their Christian faith and practice. Is it possible to be a 'good Christian' and yet not go, or at least not go very often, to church? What would such a model of faith look like? And if we find, as I believe we do, examples of it, is it something that should be encouraged for its own sake, or is the entirety of our mission effort to be directed towards increasing congregational membership? To put it bluntly, are we in mission to help people become, and become better, disciples of Jesus, or to help them become, and become better, committed members of our regular worshipping community?

The final chapter in this section is something of a 'worked example'. I've taken a look at how Church of England congregations who wish to receive Holy Communion on more frequent occasions than the pattern of availability of the vicar, or any other priest attached to their parish, seek to respond to the Church's official option of 'Communion by Extension'. More specifically, I've shown how what is actually going on in the middle of often difficult negotiations and arguments is a very good example of all four of the dimensions of the belonging model coming into play.

The second part of the book turns the spotlight more deliberately onto people who come to church, but only occasionally. Following the model of the previous section I want to think of the ways in which people, places and single events mediate for them a sense of Christian belonging. We will try to look at them not as those who are lukewarm in their faith, or simply less committed than you or me. The first chapter, in particular, will seek to dispel the notion that they are just practitioners of 'Christianity-Lite', by examining their beliefs and attitudes. The following chapter takes us explicitly into the area of the Anglican *Five Marks of Mission* to which I referred at the beginning. When I first began to write the paper behind the chapter, it was intended to explore how a local church might engage with occasional churchgoers as the recipients of mission. But the more I reflected, and the more I looked at what I had been discovering through the development of my model of belonging, the more I became convinced that this was missing the most important point. People who engage with the Christian faith and its local community through people, places and single events are not just the object of our mission but are also co-workers with us in carrying it out. Indeed, it may well be that engaging them in mission work is a far better way of enabling them to grow in their faith than seeing them exclusively as on the receiving end of our efforts.

The final chapter of this section began to emerge as I was putting together a collection of my writings as part of the process of being awarded a research doctorate. It offers another worked example. This time it is about the ways in which both the governance model for the Church of England, and the ways in which the Church is financed, have moved over time in a direction that places responsibility and power almost exclusively in the hands of those who belong in one particular of our four modes.

The third section of the book takes us beyond the fourfold belonging model in order to look at some of the other ways in which particular sorts of people may be less numerically present in churches than we ought to expect. We will take a look first at the notion of Psychological Type, familiar to many clergy at least through the popular Myers-Briggs Type Indicator®, and then go on to explore a somewhat less well-known but important topic, the concept of Religious Orientation. I'm indebted to my research colleagues, especially the Revd Canon Professor Leslie Francis, who have studied these concepts in other places and kindly allowed me to add to my Worcester Carol Service survey the specially designed and tested sets of questions that are used, in order to assess them in ways that are both statistically reliable but don't make the questionnaire too long to complete. As in earlier sections, I will want to look at who is less often to be found in church. Because the same questions have been asked of other, regular Sunday church congregations, there's also the opportunity to explore whether or not carol services offer a wider or different appeal. The nature of the concepts that we are dealing with in these chapters means that this is probably the part of the book that has the most numbers in it. But even here it is the arguments that matter; the numbers are principally there to back them up. Once again, the section will conclude with a worked example. In this case I want to focus on the implications for Sunday worship of having an awareness of the differences in Type and Orientation that exist among Christians.

Although I enjoy study, I don't pretend to be an academic. The decision I took back in 1979, and which thankfully the Church of England endorsed, to leave the world of research and become a clergyman instead, was clear and permanent. What I am, like many Christian clergy, is a 'reflective practitioner'. I try to think about the people I meet and the situations I find myself and my church in, and to do so using the best tools available to me. Writing down what I have been thinking about, and submitting it to the test of publication in the academic press, is part of what helps me to ensure my reasoning is as clear and accurate as I can make it. But my principle aim is to support and encourage the work of the Church in mission and ministry. To that end you will find in the chapters that follow plenty of examples of how things are working and how they might be made to work better. I'd be disappointed if many people read this book without at some point coming across an idea that they would want to try out in their own church or context. When you do come across such ideas, I hope the book might also provide hints as to what you might have to do to make them happen, and some of the reasons why you might find yourself meeting obstacles and objections along the way. I've set out three or four questions at the end of each chapter, which may help to focus your thoughts, especially if you are reading this book as part of a group. All in all it is about how churches might move to a better informed ministry. It's about paying attention and listening to the people God has placed around us, either directly or by using research tools. It's about trying to make our mission a bit more incarnational. It's about how, in this particular aspect of our being the Church, we imitate Christ.

Questions

- Do you think that William Temple's statement about the Church is true?

- How relevant is it to the call of the Church today?

- How much does it matter if Christian churches only reflect a part of the wider population?

- Is it important to understand how people differ?

Part One How we belong

Chapter 1

Belonging:
a theological concept

Belonging and the scriptures

From a Christian perspective our prime 'belonging' relationship is with God. And our Bibles would suggest that's a pretty wide and comprehensive idea.

The Old Testament notion of the 'People of God' is the best developed corporate understanding of what it is to belong. Without, at that stage in Israel's journey, a consistent and developed sense of an afterlife, it is the present belonging with God rather than the promise of a future destiny that lies to the fore of much of the Hebrew scriptures. It's a belonging that is expressed in many ways. We first come across it strongly in a series of covenants between God and humanity, set in the times of figures such as Noah, Abraham and Moses. This belonging is often sealed with a visible sign: in Noah's case it is to be the rainbow; for Abraham it lies in the ritual of circumcision. Alongside this belonging with the whole of humanity, or with a race or nation, the Old Testament stories are full of examples of how God belongs with particular individuals. In two cases, Enoch and Elijah, they are taken directly into God's presence without experiencing death. Key to all these examples is the idea that belonging is not unidirectional but mutual. 'We are your people and you are our God.' It rises through the Old Testament and reaches a crescendo in the poetic and erotic language of the Song of Songs, where the lover and the beloved express the depth of the passion of a belonging summed up briefly in the phrase, 'My beloved is mine and I am his' (Song of Solomon 2:16).

When we move on to look at the New Testament, we find that both the individual and corporate aspects of belonging with God are developed further. The role of Jesus, as the one who mediates belonging between human beings and the Father, stands particularly prominent in the Gospel stories set around the events of the first Easter. Matthew, Mark and Luke all emphasise the significance of Jesus inviting his followers to partake of his body and his blood, a theme that St Paul picks up in his first letter to Corinth. Those who eat and drink in this way are joined to one another and to Christ. St John takes a slightly different tack, though again he is focused on the events of the night in which Jesus was to be arrested. In his case, it is the mutual indwelling of the Father and the Son in love, into which the disciples are invited to join, that is the key message. In the Acts of the Apostles, as well as in Paul's epistles, we gain a sense of how baptism is becoming a crucial rite, both creating and expressing belonging with God, and is as unrepeatable as circumcision. Meanwhile, the complex relationship between Jesus, the earliest Christian community and the Jerusalem temple is played out across the pages of the four Gospels and Acts.

There is much in the scriptures, then, which speaks of human belonging with God, and which sees this as expressed in a far richer set of ways than simply in the sort of frequent and regular cultic activities that individuals and communities may participate in. But if we are to look beyond regular churchgoers, how wide can we cast our net?

It's a question to which there are two standard but very different answers. The subtitle of Grace Davie's influential book *Believing without Belonging*[1] suggests that we might be interested in those people who hold to a doctrinal faith, but choose not to translate it into participating membership. The problem lies in coming to any clear position on what comprises a sufficient level of belief in order to qualify. The survey forms I've produced and analysed invite respondents to signify agreement or otherwise with statements on the one hand as broad as, 'I believe in God' and, 'I believe in Jesus Christ', and on the other as specific as, 'I believe that God made the world in six days and rested on the seventh' and, 'I believe that Jesus really turned water into wine'. They are important questions to ask, and I'll come back to them later on, but they have two major drawbacks. One problem is that the relationship between the answers that people give to these questions and their actual involvement in church life is more complex than we might at first imagine. However, my greater concern is that doctrinally based criteria are by their very nature imposed on those who we are studying, and seeking to engage with, from the outside. The alternative, and the route I much prefer, is to put the ball back in the court of the individuals themselves and invite them simply to define themselves as Christian if they so wish.

There are some who see such 'self-defined Christian affiliation' as at best a potential for being drawn into a 'proper' faith, and others who consider it as a hindrance to or vaccination against evangelism. Against these views Thomas, in his book *Counting People In*,[2] distinguishes between 'participant' and 'associate' membership and warns the Church against a policy of working solely to maintain the former whilst ignoring the latter. He remarks on how people choose to identify with 'brands and ideas' rather than 'groups and meetings' and notes that successful organisations are often those that 'enable us to support them without requiring our participation in the organisations themselves'.

My stance is that belonging is sufficiently powerful as a theological concept to demand the Church pays full attention to it, both responding appropriately to its manifestations and promoting it at various levels of its work. By doing so, the Christian belonging of far more people than the small percentage of the population who attend a church on Sundays, or even that wider group who subscribe to somebody else's definition of an adequate doctrinal framework, can be both described and nurtured.

Reflecting on this wider concept of how human beings and communities belong with God has led me to identify four different aspects of Christian belonging: belonging with people, activities, events and places. It is this model that flows through this book. In the following four chapters I will be looking to explain and illustrate these four more fully; before that, it may be helpful to describe each of them as briefly as possible, as they emerged via the scriptures, into the life of the early Church, and on to our present generation.

Belonging with people

The children of Israel belong, in the Old Testament, not only with God but with each other. The Jewish Law seeks to manage this belonging, and the prophets repeatedly call the people to repentance for failing to maintain the standards of justice that such belonging requires. Several of the later epistles in the New Testament pick up the secular model, in Roman-influenced society, of a 'household', built around a network of interpersonal relationships. They adapt and adopt it in order to construct the emerging notion of a church, with bishops, presbyters and deacons who both lead the community and model the Christian life for others. Several major denominations still define themselves as being those in communion with a particular senior bishop.

Within the Christian community, the church has its lay and ordained ministers and officers. These are individuals who are associated in the minds of those they meet with the church. What they do is seen, to a greater or lesser extent, as the church doing it. Some hold formal office, as clergy, churchwardens, readers or members of a local ministry team. Others are simply recognised for what they do: visiting, flower-arranging, organising events or by virtue of their having previously occupied some such role.

Belonging with people offers a route in for those who for reasons of time or distance are not taking part in regular activities. For some, the most significant way of sustaining their belonging as part of the church is through key people visiting them, or inviting them to visit in turn. Regular letters, parish magazines or telephone conversations can also have a part to play. For some individuals with complex working patterns, it may be more practicable to retain relationships with significant individuals than to fit in with the relatively less flexible diary demands of attending a regular activity.

Belonging through relationship does, of course, give rise to the potential for conflict. My belonging may be at the expense of yours. Conflicts may arise through personality clashes or may be the consequences of competition between individuals for recognition, authority and status. One commonly cited example is of tension when new arrivals in a parish bring with them skills and enthusiasm to run things. Those who have been previously accustomed to being seen at the heart of the church community may express genuine gratitude for the new energy of the incomers whilst at the same time feeling marginalised by them.

Belonging with activities

Activity, as it is understood today, is much less to the fore in the Bible. The Old Testament has its daily temple rituals performed by priests, but there is little that speaks of demands on individual Israelites for frequent and regular participation. However, by the time of Jesus the synagogue is a significant locus for activity, and the early disciples quickly pick up the pattern of weekly observance that remains familiar today. Paul's various lists of spiritual gifts attest to a range of individuals regularly applying their skills to further the regular life of the church.

Activities are those things that take place on a regular and frequent basis, and where individuals are expected to engage not just on a specific occasion but with the series. So, for example, Sunday services, youth groups, home fellowships, Mothers' Union, toddler groups and the Parochial Church Council meetings are examples of church-run activities; by contrast, Christmas services, baptisms, funerals, garden fetes and concerts are categorised here as events.

Taking part in activities requires a significant investment of time and energy. It is not unusual in a parish to find the same individuals maintaining a variety of them, both within the church and in the wider community. It is often those who like activities who run the events, maintain the buildings and act as the significant individuals in the community. Some activity-led people grumble that others don't join in as much as they should, and may even doubt the genuineness of a belonging that isn't activity based. Many church activities are not contested, since those who don't wish to involve themselves don't have to take part. However, when it comes to the timings and style of Sunday worship, where there is a sense of the broadest range of the Christian community gathering for a shared act, then there is always the potential for what best sustains my sense of belonging being what is least helpful for you.

Belonging with events

The notion of expressing religious belonging through events is evident in the various covenant makings of ancient Israel as well as in the rites for circumcision, purification of women and cleansing of lepers. In the early Church these are superseded by baptism as the main event-based expression of religious affiliation. The notion of affirming religious identity at a variety of rites of passage, such as confirmation and first communion, builds on this over successive centuries.

Most churches undertake a range of events that engender belonging. The occasional offices of baptisms, marriages and funerals are a crucial part of them. They express a belonging with the Church and with God at key moments in the lives of the individuals directly concerned. They place the church at the centre of how a network of friends, relatives and neighbours expresses its belonging together. Along with these, major festivals such as Christmas and Harvest allow a belonging with the Christian story to be expressed and enacted. Concerts, fetes, garden parties and social events offer a belonging together in the community, with the church acknowledged as having an explicit part in that belonging.

Some communities engender a significant amount of belonging

through secular events that are not part of an organisation with wider aims. The well dressings of rural Derbyshire and the Open Garden weekends of Worcestershire are examples. Often the church or its core membership plays a central role in arranging and promoting such events. They illustrate that there can be two levels of belonging going on at the same time. There is a basic level of belonging, with both the local community and the place, which is offered to those who visit the events. At the same time, there is a deeper sense of belonging engendered in many of those who plan and deliver such occasions.

Because they are essentially 'one-off' events, they allow a different and wider range of people to be involved. They are not the main aspect of belonging for those who are activists, some of whom disparage event-based belonging. However, they often offer the main way of belonging to longer term residents who are not otherwise active.

Public events such as fetes allow individuals to express support without making an ongoing commitment. Tourists and visitors are often drawn to them. One of the trickiest issues may be identifying appropriate means of communication, so that those who would want to come know that the event is happening. Churches are traditionally poor at maintaining contact with those who live outside of the parish unless they are regular worshippers.

Occasional offices are legally public but are seen by most as essentially private affairs, directed towards the invited guests of those concerned. Each of these rites brings with it areas of contention. The practice of pressing for baptisms to be held during a regular Sunday main service is a good example of the activist seeking to enforce their own understanding on event belongers. The residence requirements within the marriage preliminaries threaten the belonging of some who cannot satisfy very specific criteria. Clergy who use their discretion not to offer Archbishop's Licences, or who restrict the availability of marriage services in the case where a participant is divorced are also denying belonging, as are those who refuse the funerals of non-residents. This is not said in order to suggest that such restrictions are always wrong, but simply to recognise that the pastoral practice of a parish or its incumbent has missional consequences that need to be given an appropriate degree of weight alongside other theological and discipleship factors.

Belonging with places

The importance of the land in ancient Israel has been explored in detail by the theologian Walter Brueggemann. He identifies that the Old Testament 'was not all about deeds, but was concerned with place, specific real estate that was invested with powerful promises', and describes the 'dialectic in Israel's fortunes between landlessness (wilderness, exile) and landedness, the latter either as possession of the land, as anticipation of the land or as grief about loss of the land'.[3]

The notion of Jerusalem as a place of especial significance to the whole nation pervades the Jewish scriptures. And yet, at an individual level, above all other land there is a special relationship with the particular place where someone lives. The Jubilee laws of Leviticus 25 cover the purchase and sale of domestic properties, distinguishing carefully between homes in walled towns and those in villages or open countryside. Whilst place features less centrally in the New Testament, the early Church soon begins to hallow particular locations, such as the sites of martyrdoms. Meanwhile, the eschatological vision of the heavenly Jerusalem in the Revelation of St John draws Christians to identify themselves with a future place that is their destiny.

In many communities, especially in more rural areas, the church and churchyard are the most significant places in terms of contributing to belonging. Such churches are almost invariably the oldest, or among the oldest, buildings in the area. One of their functions is to stand as a symbol of permanence amidst a society of change. That permanence looks backwards, in providing a sense of belonging to the heritage of the community—and makes the church the natural location for memorials to significant persons, institutions or events. It also looks forwards, for example, expressing in stone and wood the permanence that a couple are seeking when they make their marriage vows.

The parish church is in many cases the visual symbol of the identity of the community; very often it will feature prominently on the community website and on local memorabilia. Parish churches are seen by many outside the Christian faith as being 'spiritual space'. They use the church as somewhere holy to come and be quiet whilst they undertake their own spiritual journey, which does not recognise a need for liturgies, doctrine or ministers. The churchyard affirms the belonging both of those who lie beneath its surface and of the community who remember them. Indeed, the expectation that it will be there in future to receive one's own remains is something that offers belonging to the living.

Belonging with the place is often the most important tie for those who are not resident. It is also the point where the wider belonging by the public in general is asserted; a belonging very often made visible during concerns over the preservation of heritage. The Church of England's faculty jurisdiction system recognises a range of individuals whose belonging with the Church must be taken into account, giving them rights of petition and objection to any significant change. Diocesan Advisory Committees include representation from the amenity societies representing a range of specific interests. National heritage bodies combine the dual roles of both offering critical comment on proposals and providing core funding for restoration work. This heritage role may conflict with the understandable desires of the present congregation to make the building congenial for present uses, and to economise on construction costs.

There is a link between belonging with place and belonging with events in that place. Events are for many the primary way through which belonging to place is expressed. The church building which has hosted generations of a family's rites of passage is hallowed by that history and also by the promise of its future availability. However, it is important not to collapse places back into events. Schemes for the internal reordering of churches, to make both activities and events more comfortable, and more resonant with current worship styles, often fall foul of this. Once a place has become sacred, then any alteration to it runs the risk of being seen as sacrilege. A good demonstration that it is the building rather than the event which carries this status can be seen in the much more positive attitude that those who belong through place or event are seen to have with regard to modern liturgies, not least to wedding marches and funeral music, than to the reordering of buildings.

Place belonging in the churchyard can be contentious when space is short and restrictive criteria are introduced. But by far the most frequent cause of conflict is over monuments. Having the gravestone one wants, in the churchyard one wants it and being able to plant, tend, edge or otherwise mark out the grave space plays a central role in many a grieving family's assertion of belonging with their deceased. However, a totally unregulated graveyard, subject both to the whims of individuals and competitive demonstrations of mourning, detracts from the belonging of the wider community, including the heritage interests.

Testing the concept

This chapter has set out a theological model for belonging and described its four main aspects. We've had a quick look at some of the issues that arise in practice, and seen that the model allows us a lens through which we can see into some of the conflicts that arise when belonging is contested. In the next four chapters I want to look at each of these types of belonging in more detail. But, before I do so, let me describe how the evidence used in those chapters, and indeed through the rest of this book, was gathered.

In the autumn of 2007 I asked a number of churches in rural parts of Worcestershire to distribute and collect a survey form during their Harvest Festival services. Some 27 agreed, and from these I received almost 1500 completed questionnaires. I had invited respondents to give me basic demographic information and then to tell me how often they attended church, and how frequently they said their prayers. After this, they were asked a wide series of questions about their connections with the local church and the community, about their religious beliefs and attitudes and about why they had come to the service.

A second questionnaire was used a couple of years later at the two main Christmas carol services in Worcester Cathedral and repeated the following year in Lichfield. This repeated the basic demographic details along with asking about motivations for attending. It went on to ask more specific questions about beliefs in the Christmas story alongside general religious beliefs and practices. The Worcester version of the survey also contained a Psychological Type instrument and one for determining Religious Orientation.

For both surveys all the adults present were given the questionnaire and a pencil before the service began, and invited to complete and return it before leaving church. Harvest and Christmas were chosen both because it was likely, and indeed proved to be the case, that the congregations would include a fair number of people who were not regular churchgoers, and also because on such occasions people will tend to arrive earlier and have more time to complete the survey before the worship begins.

Questions

- Are there one or two particular stories from the scriptures in this chapter that appeal to me? Why might they affect me in this way?

- Am I happy with considering as Christian those who choose to define themselves as such but have no commitment to regular churchgoing?

- Which of people, places, events and activities is most important to me in my own belonging to God?

Chapter 2

Reliably regular: belonging through church activities

Becoming a Christian, at the age of 17, was the easy thing. I had a strong conviction that Jesus had indeed risen from the dead, and this was bolstered by the fact that the one whom I encountered in my prayers was recognisably the same as the one of whom I read in the Gospel narratives. Forty years on, I'm more convinced than ever. The harder part was joining a church. But I had a strong sense that this was what Christians did, and so I put up with the strangeness of liturgy, the poor quality of community singing, the unfamiliar layout of church buildings and the tediousness of many sermons. It wasn't made any easier by my spending half the year at university and the other half at home. But I'm a persistent type and eventually became encultured to churchgoing. I grew to enjoy both Sunday worship and midweek fellowship or study groups. When I felt God calling me to ordained ministry, I knew that this wasn't simply because of my gifts and strengths, but also because of my weaknesses. If I was to be committed to Christ, it would need to be in a way that impacted on all of my life; one that shaped how I spent the vast majority of my time, that gave me routines and habits around which everything else would fall into place. I wasn't sure I was up to the demands of holding a secular career and being a committed follower of Jesus Christ at the same time.

Also, I'm a natural joiner-in. All voluntary organisations, not least the Church, need people like me. We commit ourselves to regular activities. We give up our free time to serve on committees and groups in order to plan and deliver the organisation's programme. We dig into our pockets, or better still, make a regular commitment from our bank account, in order to fund not just special initiatives that have caught our imagination, but regular overheads and core costs. We are those who, in the model introduced in the previous chapter, belong through activities.

My Harvest research findings showed that people who are active in the local church are also more likely to be active in other community organisations. The same people run the local cricket club, sit on the civil parish council, organise weekly lunches for the elderly and form the backbone of the congregation and church council.

One afternoon, in the mid-1990s, the leader of my Mothers' Union branch came to see me about an idea they had had. They had noticed that there was another organisation in the parish, the Townswomen's Guild, which attracted a similar demographic to themselves: active older women who enjoyed regular meetings with others, including listening to a speaker and sharing refreshments. They reasoned that this would be a group who would be naturally amenable to joining the MU, and then from the MU to becoming regular churchgoers. They were absolutely right. For the next few years there was a steady trickle of confirmation candidates who had followed that route and become regular members of the weekly congregation. It was a splendid example of activity-based outreach.

The pattern we have inherited, of the same people going weekly, to the same service, at the same time and in the same place, has served Christian denominations in Britain very well in previous generations. But it is a pattern that has steadily been breaking down over the last 50 years. One of the earliest developments was the Family Service. Often in more recent times rebranded as All Age Worship so as to emphasise that it isn't aimed purely at those with young children, the pattern grew and proliferated to one Sunday morning a month when the worship would have a distinctive style and content, and would be meant to be particularly child-friendly. In some parishes, including my own, the uniformed organisations (Scouts, Guides etc.) would be invited to attend dressed as for their own meetings, and their flags would be paraded at the start and end of the service. Strong use was made of the seasons of the year. A programme built around services for Mothering

Sunday, Easter, Harvest, Remembrance and Christmas was padded out with less obvious themes for the intervening months. The aim was clear, to build a group of people who had a commitment to monthly worship, which might for some lead on to their becoming members of the congregation on 'ordinary' Sundays too.

Such services are now a mainstay of the worship pattern of many Anglican parishes. They are often the best attended service of the month and the relative informality of their style has provided a context in which lay worship leaders can develop and practise skills. Crucially, they created a framework in which churchgoing did not need to be a weekly habit, as long as it was sufficiently frequent to instil a sense of commitment not just to the specific event being attended, but to the series of which it formed a part. The academic consensus seems to be that the change from turning up for a 'one-off' event and feeling a sense of belonging to a regular series of occasions occurs at around the six times a year mark. If we attend something more often than once every two months, then we develop a commitment to the sequence, not just the individual service.

The pattern of determinedly going to church every Sunday, which I was making myself commit to in the mid-1970s, was already beginning to be challenged through changes taking place in wider society. New employment patterns meant that people began to live further away from the rest of their families, and to use their recently acquired motor vehicles to spend some Sundays visiting. Sports events began to spill from Saturdays into Sundays, leisure facilities started to open and eventually Sunday trading legislation was considerably relaxed. At the same time the growth in divorce and remarriage meant that many children did not spend every weekend with the same parent, whilst increased longevity turned weekends into times for caring for elderly parents living at a distance. Increased disposable income led to people taking more weekend breaks away from home. Changes in working patterns resulted in many more people having to work on at least some Sundays of the month. The Family Service itself created a group of churchgoers who didn't like it and would either attend a different service or church that Sunday, or not go to church at all.

In consequence of this, regular churchgoing today, for many of the most committed to it, is not a strict weekly pattern, but probably averages out at between two and three Sundays per month.

The Family Service was indeed an early and widespread example, but over the last decade or so, especially since the publication of *Mission-shaped Church*,[4] we have seen a proliferation of fresh expressions of church and of variations in the patterns of worship both on Sundays and at other times. What the vast majority of these have in common, from Café Church via Messy Church and on to church worship taking place in coffee shops, is that they seek to sustain Christian life through commitment to a regular, but usually not weekly, worship activity; possibly augmented by smaller group gatherings on separate occasions. Some are run under the oversight of a traditional church leadership, but others have a considerable degree of autonomy.

A key insight of the Fresh Expressions movement is that the services that take place are not to be seen as stepping stones towards some sort of 'real' church of a more traditional nature; they are fully church in their own right. Nor are they to be seen as augmentations of worship, provided to help those who hang on in with the 'normal' style of Sunday worship, but who need something extra and more captivating once in a while. To be a member of a fresh expression is to be as much a part of the Church as to be a member of a traditional form.

So far this chapter has looked at how we belong through activities that bring us into face-to-face contact with other Christians. For many Christians, however, that forms only a minority part of how they practise their faith. Alongside going to church, one of the things that seemed clear to me from the moment my faith first came alive was that it should also be rooted in regular private devotional practice. My first attempt was to read my Authorised Version Bible, the only one I owned, from cover to cover. I read about a dozen chapters of Genesis in the first day, three or four the next day, just a single chapter the day after that, and then faltered completely. At the back of a church I came across a set of Bible Reading Fellowship notes. Each day had a short passage printed out in an easy-to-follow translation, with alongside it a paragraph of explanatory notes. The discipline of having the date above each section, together with the knowledge that other people would be reading the same passage in their own homes, made all the difference. This was just sufficient structure to hold me to task, as well as just enough information to make the passage interesting without my feeling I was being treated to somebody's sermon every day. The rhythm not only helped me to read and understand the Bible, it also created a fixed point in the day that I was able to make a focus for my prayers as well.

In the last few years we have begun to see a huge increase in structures set up to support a disciplined devotional life. Some of this has been as part of the growth in interest in forms of dispersed religious community. One element often to be found in these emerging bodies is that the members share a common structure for a Rule or Rhythm of Life. Within the community each individual may tailor the details of that Rule to fit their specific circumstances, but there is both a shared framework and a sense of accountability to the other members of the community for keeping it. In some communities that accountability is formalised through each member having to submit an annual report into how they have fared, as well as through the expectation that each will have a spiritual director or companion, to whom they are giving account on a more frequent (typically quarterly) basis. Historically, such Rules have been common among oblates of traditional monastic communities, and for groups such as Franciscan Tertiaries. What is new is that many of the emerging Rhythm of Life groups have no connection to any Order from within the inherited monastic tradition. Some are coming into being at diocesan level, such as the Community of St Chad in Lichfield and the Peregrini Community in Manchester; others are happening at as local a basis as a single parish. Alongside the Rhythm, some such communities have produced their own short Daily Prayer offices, recognising that saying the same words on the same day, even if the members are all doing it independently and at different times, itself enhances the sense of belonging both to the community and then to the God whom it exists to worship and to serve. Inevitably, some are beginning to use webcams and internet communications services in order to join in saying the community prayers together—able to hear each others' voices and see their faces—even whilst doing so from their own homes.

We can see, then, that Christian belonging through activities has changed considerably as the range of activities through which such belonging can be mediated has proliferated. An individual church may well contain a range of people who are accessing different patterns and styles of worship. For the individual churchgoer, however, it means that their belonging through activities may be built up from a range of components, not all accessed from the same structure. So, for example, I may belong to a Sunday congregation, where I attend worship at least a couple of times a month, yet seek to avoid one particular Sunday when the style is not to my liking. Alongside this, I may be a member of a fortnightly justice and peace or Bible study group that draws people from several denominations in my community. I won't get to every meeting, because of my work commitments, but I feel part of the group and know that the others there consider me to be a member. In addition, I sit on a church committee that meets about once every six weeks, and I usually make the effort to be there. Meanwhile, at home I have a discipline of prayer and Bible study which I share with others across a widely dispersed area and whom I meet only occasionally face-to-face.

In my experience, churches are often on their strongest ground when it comes to creating, enhancing and sustaining a varied programme of regular public activities that will broaden their reach beyond what could be served by a more monochrome format. I suspect that at least in part this is because the sort of people who will give up their time to serve on the church councils and committees that come up with, and oversee, such activities are people for whom making regular commitments goes with their natural grain. We wouldn't serve on the church committee if we weren't that sort of person. The most challenging aspect is about broadening the reach. There is a natural human tendency to assume that if we as a church do what I myself like best, and do it really well, then this will attract others. It's also quite a safe attitude to hold, because its success will only make me feel more at home in the church, not less.

One of my greatest challenges as a parish priest was in leading a church that was growing in directions that made some of its members, including myself, feel less that our particular preferred style was at the heart of our worship. I had to broaden my own appreciation of the range of Anglican churchmanship and spirituality. Others did too. We held together and then continued to grow, but it was hard. Around the same time I remember a friend telling me that he and his wife had left their local church and found somewhere else; not because their former parish was doing the wrong thing—they agreed wholly with the direction of its outreach and mission—but they had just recognised that it was not what would sustain them.

Perhaps, though, the greater challenge in how to enhance belonging through regular activity lies in the support provided for the individual devotional life of church members. Whilst I have found in my studies that both regular Bible reading and frequent private prayer are strongly associated with more frequent churchgoing, the levels of both are still quite low among even the most committed. Some churches will have the capacity to create a local Rule or Rhythm, to invite members to sign up to it and to support them with appropriate materials. For others there may be much to be gained from exploring the availability of wider dispersed communities, either diocesan or otherwise.

Questions

- What regular church activities are most important to me?

- Am I someone who finds it easy to make and keep regular commitments?

- Are there particular sorts of church activities that I find it harder to commit myself to, and why?

- Can somebody be a 'regular' churchgoer if they only attend worship once a month?

Chapter 3

People power: belonging through relationships

Let me introduce you to Mavis. Mavis was churchwarden in one of the villages of which I was incumbent. Until retirement she had taught in the local primary school, which was no more than half a mile from her home. She had been a Sunday school teacher until, with the changes to Sunday sport and shopping laws in the 1980s, the numbers had no longer been viable. It seemed like the whole village knew her, and knew her as a person at the heart of the local church. People loved her dearly, and would do almost anything that she asked. But it went further than that; I found that people looked to and identified with Mavis as a way of looking to and identifying with God. Somehow, being close to her helped those who knew her feel closer to God.

Mavis isn't the only person who has represented Christian belonging to me in that way. Back when I was a young student at theological college, I was helping out in a parish in a part of inner-city Birmingham. One of my roles was to visit people living in a street that had recently been rebuilt after slum clearance. Doing so, I came across a woman who was entirely housebound. On a good day she could get out of bed and sit for a few hours in her chair. Most days she suffered so many epileptic fits that she was safer lying down. People from an amazingly diverse range of backgrounds would pop round to visit her. The attraction was simply that she prayed for people, and prayed in a way that made me, and others, really conscious that here was somebody very close to God. Being in her house was like being in church. Meeting her made us all that little bit closer to God ourselves. If I remember it rightly, the bishop came over and confirmed her in her bedroom.

It is experiences like these that have convinced me that an important part of our Christian belonging, even our belonging with God, is mediated through the belonging we experience with specific other people. That shouldn't be surprising; after all, the Bible states very clearly that human beings are created in God's image. When we look at another person, we are looking at an image of God. Some of us may be better at recognising that image than others. St Francis of Assisi, in his early adult years when he was still struggling to discover his calling, set off on horseback for a journey. A short distance along his way he met a leper standing in the middle of the track and begging. Like many of his generation, Francis was both frightened and disgusted by the sight of the disfigurements associated with the disease. Yet he dismounted, approached the man and embraced him. Not long after, Francis and his first companions were to be found running a refuge for lepers. Francis had seen the face of Christ in the face of the suffering man; in embracing the human, he was embracing the divine. The early, rapid growth of the Franciscan movement was, I am convinced, fuelled by the fact that when people were close to Francis, they knew they were also close to God.

Moreover, Trinitarian Christians subscribe to the view that there is relationship even within God himself. Father, Son and Holy Spirit are bound together in a mutual intimacy and love that has existed from before the act of creation began and, as St Paul reminds us memorably in chapter 13 of his first letter to Corinth, love is one of the few things that are truly eternal. Human beings are invited, not simply to aspire to be with God in heaven, but to live our lives in relationship with him here and now, and to make that relationship the fixed centre point of our existence in a world of rapid, often discontinuous, change. God calls us to relate with him, and gives us one another as part of the means through which that relationship is supported and strengthened.

There's plenty of ground, then, in terms of scripture, theology and examples drawn from present-day life, on which to assert that this relational dimension, belonging through people, is a solid aspect of what it is to be a Christian. In the next part of this chapter I'd like to introduce you to what the 1450 respondents to my Worcestershire

Harvest service survey made of it. The Harvest Sunday survey congregations contained quite a lot of people who are not frequent churchgoers, around a fifth of them attending approximately monthly and another quarter less often than that. For the purposes of study, I divided belonging through people into three aspects, to which I gave the names Congregational Belonging, Pastoral Support and Personal Intimacy. The survey contained three or four questions about each.

When I put to people whether they agreed with the statement that 'This is my "family" church', two-thirds answered positively, less than a tenth disagreed. The figures were broadly similar for the next statement: 'I have a strong sense of belonging to this church community.' Meanwhile, almost a half agreed that 'I come to church to be with other people', with only one in six disagreeing. In other words, many of us find that an important aspect of our Congregational Belonging in church is through the other people who are either there when we come, or are people whom we associate with the church.

I want to affirm this dimension of belonging, and to do so strongly. People, including a significant proportion who are not regular congregation members, feel they belong to the church community and have a sense that this belonging goes beyond their individual relationship to embrace their wider family. They see the other people present at worship as an important and welcome aspect of what they come to be part of. Belonging through people is, however, two-edged. Positively, it can be the spur to an inclusive welcome, forming a church community that builds links between unlikely neighbours and drives social outreach into the neediest parts of the community. Conversely, it can be the motivation for a church having a 'club' mentality. Coming to church to 'be with other people' can mean that I want the congregation to be made up of people who look and behave in very similar ways to me and who share my wider interests and my outlook on life. I've heard tales of parishes turning down an opportunity for outreach on the basis that, 'We don't want that sort of person coming here.' Less overtly, it can be expressed in a welcome that is very much 'on our terms', in which new people are able to join and feel included in the church as long as they always remember who the dominant group are, and do nothing to challenge that dominance.

The second area of belonging through people is that of Personal Intimacy. I wanted to explore the extent to which people have friendships at church and how well they feel known, both by others in the pews and by the clergy. I was also interested in how far that sense of intimacy was dependent on the frequency of going to church. To help with this, I compared the responses of the people who claimed to go to church most weeks with those who said they attend less than monthly.

Only two per cent of the whole sample could be found to disagree with the statement, *'I have friends in this congregation'*, with four out of every five agreeing with it. Among the frequent churchgoers this figure rose to five in every six, but even among the occasional ones it only fell to just below three-quarters. People who come to church, even if they only come from time to time, find friends there. The question of whether these are friendships made in church, or friends from the wider community, is secondary. What matters is that such friendships exist for most attendees, even the infrequent ones. There's also a warning in these figures. Might it be that those who try coming to church but fail either to find existing friends there or to make new ones, don't stick?

But how deep do these relationships go? Is it simply a case of making casual acquaintanceships, or is there something stronger? My next two questions sought to explore this. The first invited respondents to react to the statement, *'I feel that people here know me well'*. Among the frequent churchgoers, two-thirds agreed, and even among the occasional attendees it was only a handful of percentage points below half. The remaining question focused specifically on the role of the lead clergyperson. Do I, or don't I *'feel that the vicar knows me well'*? The good news for clergy, especially those like me who can struggle embarrassingly to reconcile names with faces, is that over half agreed. For the most frequent churchgoers, the figure went up to 60 per cent; for the less regular it dropped, but was still more than a third.

Many of the people attending Harvest services in Church of England parishes, even among those who don't come to church often, clearly felt well known. The figures are not so high as to suggest that those who prefer privacy, people who come to church to commune only with God and otherwise want to keep themselves to themselves, have no place to hide. However, they are high enough to indicate that the sense of being well known is a significant part of the experience of churchgoing for most people, even for many who attend infrequently. For those who are relatively rare visitors to church services it suggests that Anglican congregations, and their clergy, are good at getting out and about in the community. Many occasional churchgoers feel that both church members and the vicar know them, and know them well. Given that quite a number of the 27 churches that took part in the survey were part of parishes or benefices with several church buildings, this is a remarkable tribute to the strength of the network of social relationships that churches contain.

Personal intimacy forms the potential ground for Pastoral Support, the third area explored in the questionnaire. Given that the previous answer showed many people holding a strong sense of being well known, would it be the case that this had a practical impact for them in times of need? I invited the survey participants to indicate whether they receive help from other people in the church, by responding to the phrase: *'There are people here who help me cope with things.'* Around half agreed with the statement and only one in eight disagreed. That suggests that there are a lot of people who cannot answer the question directly, probably because the situation of needing such support hasn't arisen. Of the rest, it would seem most likely that the ability and willingness of the church to provide such support is being strongly affirmed. The figure is likely to be skewed a little towards the positive side, if those who have looked for pastoral support and not found it have then left the congregation to look elsewhere, but turnover rates for church membership are not so high as to suggest this would account for what we've found.

Within the field of pastoral care, a lot of interest is paid to the subject of visiting by churches. Most newly appointed clergy are soon exposed to tales of the wonderful incumbent from some previous decade who visited everybody regularly. What I found was that 42 per cent of people claim to be visited in their home by *'people from this church'*, with just a quarter being visited by *'the vicar'* and about one in seven by *'another church leader'*. This suggests that clerical home visits now play a relatively minor role in sustaining the pattern of church belonging for most churchgoers, regular or occasional. It also would fit with a view that clergy visiting now mostly falls into one of two categories. The first are visits either in reaction to, or anticipation of, some event. These would include visiting the sick, preparation for weddings and funerals etc. and responding to pastoral crises. Other visits are most likely to be centred on those who are actively involved in delivering the church's ministry: churchwardens, Readers, licensed or authorised lay ministers, leaders of church groups of one kind or another. In rural areas, and increasingly in urban ones too, the vicar's role is moving from being almost exclusively one of direct one-to-one engagement to a delicate balance between personal action and the oversight of others. The evidence from the Harvest survey would appear to be that clergy are successfully negotiating this transition without a perception that they have been forced by workload to withdraw from direct engagement so far that they no longer know their people well. It may also suggest that the community role of the vicar, being visible at social events and elsewhere, remains strong enough to sustain a sense of belonging through being known, even without the priest undertaking individual home visits.

The responses to two further questions in the survey also shed light on the significance of relationships to the sample. Firstly, one in six agreed with the statement that they had come to the service because a friend had invited them, a figure which rose to around a quarter when the answers were restricted to those who only attend church occasionally. This confirms the importance of relationship to the evangelistic outreach of the church. It may not be the case that all people will come if they are invited, but it may well be the case that for those who do come, being a part of a relationship network with churchgoers, and being explicitly invited by one of them, makes a difference.

Secondly, almost three-quarters of the occasional churchgoing group agreed with the statement *'this church is welcoming to those who come occasionally'*, almost exactly the same percentage as among the weekly attendees. It would seem that the perception of welcome, which I hope in most cases reflects the reality, is an important part of allowing people to persist with a pattern of occasional churchgoing, rather than giving up on all church involvement.

Even for those who do not come to church frequently, this research has found significant factors around personal relationships that link such individuals to the congregation. It is highly likely that this strong network of relationships makes church a more welcoming place to those who attend infrequently. It has also highlighted the continuing role of the clergy in sustaining belonging through relationship.

Having looked at the evidence from the survey, it's now time to reflect on what it means for ordained ministers and the wider church community today.

The role of 'the vicar'

The Church of England priest is not just somebody who undertakes a series of functions set out in a job description. He or she is to be, in the best sense of the word, iconic. Many of the people who look at the vicar do so with, at least in part, the desire to look through them and to catch a glimpse of the God who is the one they are seeking to draw closer to. The way we perform the functions that we undertake may be part of what facilitates that, but it can never be sufficient. This role of icon goes far beyond that of being a good example of the Christian response to God's love and God's call. The expectation, indeed the requirement, is that clergy are, albeit in some small and poor way, examples of God's call and God's love to us.

For those of a Catholic disposition, this may be well expressed in the presidential role of the bishop or priest at the Eucharist, particularly in the predominant westward-facing position adopted in England. When I proclaim the words, 'This is my body' and 'This is my blood', with the congregation looking me square in the face from the other side of the altar, I am conscious that I am taking the part of Jesus in the drama of the institution narrative, as I also am when I pronounce the absolution of sins.

From a more evangelical perspective, it may be helpful to reflect on the fact that a word is always spoken or written by someone. When I am preaching a sermon, or engaged in a pastoral conversation or writing this book, part of what I am communicating is a relationship between myself and the listener or reader. I need to do my best to ensure that my personality doesn't become so prominent as to obscure what I am trying to communicate, but neither must I fool myself into thinking that I should try to eliminate the personal dimension entirely. What I am seeking to express should be rooted in God's word and be a reflection on it. But every act of speaking or writing that word is a little incarnation. As I have developed my own thinking in response to my research findings, I've found that I put a little more of myself and my personal journey with Christ into what I preach and write, and in how I conduct pastoral conversations. Part of how I seek to encourage people into a deeper relationship with Christ lies in helping them to form some sort of relationship, even if at a fairly cursory level, with me.

If clergy are crucial in this forming of belonging through relationship, then that has important implications for what parishes and dioceses do when the vicar moves on. As much as possible of the belonging that was being carried by the previous incumbent needs to be sustained through a period that may well involve both vacancy and pastoral reorganisation, ready for it to be built on by the next priest. Inevitably, some people will like the new vicar better than they did the old, and some vice versa. That will make a difference as to how easy or difficult they find it to belong to God's church in a particular parish, but it's something to be aware of rather than something we can do anything much about. There are, however, other aspects of clergy changes that are capable of being handled with a deliberate intention of sustaining belonging through people.

I'm regularly quizzed as to why we can't process clergy vacancies much more quickly, so that the gap between one leaving and the next arriving would be minimal. I could hide behind the law; there are legal complexities in undertaking appointments processes whilst a post is not yet vacant, but we could work around them, or even change the law, if we felt it would be a positive step. But whilst I'm no fan of vacancies that go on for a year or more, a gap of around nine months has much to be said for it. First of all, it allows those drawing up the person specification for the next priest to be able to do so after having said goodbye to the previous one. Any earlier and it's well-nigh impossible for the average church council to so far extricate itself from its relationship with its present priest that it can produce a specification that looks significantly different from them. Secondly, it allows long enough for others to become key carriers of relational belonging in the parish. Not only does this mean that the newly arrived incumbent doesn't have to automatically take all previous relationships on board, it also affords a real opportunity for other clergy and lay people to grow through the relationships that others form with them. Three different periods when, as a suffragan bishop, I was working through a vacancy or a sabbatical of my diocesan, all strengthened my relationships with other colleagues in ways that were then sustained afterwards. By contrast, there is little as destructive for relational belonging as the previous incumbent who refuses to let go. Even with the most benign intentions on all parts, it is almost impossible for a church to move on whilst the last vicar is still present on the scene or lurking on the sidelines. The mixed loyalties just don't work.

Where relationships matter there will always be the danger of factions, cliques, power struggles and personality politics. We can read of them even in the stories of Jesus and his original disciples. I suspect that ministerial training does not do enough to prepare clergy for this reality. It's also the case that a disproportionately large percentage of clergy have high levels of aversion to such conflict. For many, that's a natural consequence of the other gifts and strengths which they possess. Maybe it's a help to realise that conflicts are not a sign of weakness, but more often a sign that relationships do matter. A church that never experiences them is almost certainly relationally moribund. It's also my experience that archdeacons and others are more ready to offer help and support in such circumstances than individuals and parishes are to receive it.

Questions

- Who are the people who have been most important to me on my Christian journey, and why?

- Are there people around whom I feel closer to God, and what is it about them?

- Is there anybody for whom I appear to be a link with Christian faith?

- Is there something I could do to help others to belong more deeply to God through me?

Chapter 4

Only the once: belonging through events

My mother-in-law liked going to church. Away from home, especially when staying with us, she was always happy to come along on Sunday morning. She just wouldn't go to services in her own village. When I asked about it, she had a clear and concise rationale. If she went to church at home, 'He'll expect me there next week.' 'He' was the vicar, and I'm sure she was right. She had nothing against either the priest himself or the way they did things in her home parish, she just wasn't ready to do anything that might suggest an implied commitment to doing it again. She understood that to go even once, on an ordinary Sunday, was to open herself up to the suggestion that she should be there every week. Even if unstated, it would be in the vicar's mind, the minds of the other people in church and in her own mind too. She would somehow have been pushed into making a long-term commitment when all she wanted to do was simply to go to church on a single specific occasion, leaving the future open to whatever she might feel like then. It was only after she became a grandparent, moved to live close to us and had the excuse that she was there to help my wife with the children, that she went to church regularly enough to decide that the commitment was OK.

I learned from her example, and began, as a parish priest, to look at how we could put on and advertise church services in ways that picked some of them out as being 'one-off' occasions. We began to repackage some of our programme so that it was no longer the monthly Family Service with a Harvest (or whatever) theme, but clearly a single event. Special occasions that occur on just an annual basis lend themselves quite readily to this. The distance between Christingle or Mothering Sunday this year and the same next year is so far that any tenuous link of implied commitment is broken. We tried to make sure that those who came along to any event went home with a short flyer letting them know of future planned one-offs that were already firm in the diary. And we hoped that a small number of those who got into the habit of coming to one-off events reasonably often would eventually feel ready to come along on other occasions too, but that wasn't, explicitly or implicitly, part of the deal.

Services that the church plans as single events, and advertises to the general public, are one half of what makes for event belonging. Alongside them stand the Occasional Offices: the baptisms, weddings and funerals that take place either in the church building, or, in the case of funerals, there or the crematorium chapel. I can well understand when some clergy become jaded about such events. It's not uncommon for the guest list to include a number of people who have little rapport with the religious ceremony, and even less desire to engage worshipfully with it. But for those at the centre of the day, the occasion is a major landmark in their lives, and one that they have made a decision to undertake in a church service.

In the late 1990s, as in my three parishes we were trying to make every service more welcoming and appropriate for those attending it, the Church of England was going in the opposite direction. Revisions of the Occasional Offices, as part of the Common Worship process, seemed to be predicated on an understanding that every act of worship ought to look as much like a Sunday morning service as possible, with confessions, collects, sermon and intercessions, all following the eucharistic pattern. The Eucharist itself could be omitted, if it was felt inappropriate, but the liturgy would still broadly form the same shape. Perhaps the purpose was to make it so that if somebody present on such an occasion then turned up to regular Sunday worship they would recognise the pattern and feel more at home. However, the impression it left was that the event itself was a kind of cut-off version of worship, something intended primarily as a stepping stone to the 'real thing' and not an adequate act of Christian worship in its own right.

In preparing families for weddings, funerals and baptisms I found I was hearing a very different story. Many were seeking to express and affirm a Christian faith that might not have been visible in terms of frequency of church attendance but which had a deep place in their lives. It was important that what they were doing was being done in the presence of God, and surrounded with prayers and blessings. My later research has backed me up in this. Those who come to church, but only occasionally, are not simply present for the music, or liturgy, or the aesthetics of the location and occasion; they are genuinely expecting some sort of encounter with God when they come. That they come back again on future occasions suggests that they are not let down in their hopes.

The biblical model set out earlier supports this notion that belonging through key individual events is a valid dimension of Christian faith. Most of us can probably also identify specific occasions when that has been our own experience. When I arrived in church, actually the chapel of one of the other Cambridge colleges, for my confirmation, I was not the best-ever prepared candidate. My scheduled sessions with my own chaplain had been truncated by a death in his family. And the day itself coincided with the university Rag Week. As a keen writer of comic sketches, I had been performing with a friend in the city centre until barely an hour earlier. Other students had responded by throwing overripe tomatoes at us. There was no time to wash my hair, just a quick change of clothes, a dash to the church and a prayer that the presiding bishop would not find his hand encountering decaying vegetable matter as it approached my head. But it was an utterly memorable and profoundly holy event.

My researches into people attending one-off events in church began with my study of Harvest. I asked all the adults in the Harvest survey to indicate how often they attended the church where they were completing the questionnaire: 56 per cent reported coming nearly every week; 20 per cent at least once a month; 14 per cent at least six times a year; ten per cent fewer than six times per year. In other words, around a quarter of those present claimed to attend the church less than monthly. That these were indeed not regular churchgoers was supported by the fact that almost two-fifths of those present at the service indicated that their names were not on the church electoral roll. When we compare self-reported church attendance with congregation figures produced by ministers for denominational statistical returns, it invariably shows that people tend to claim that they go to church a little more often than is actually the case. This all suggests that the true figure of occasional attendees might, if anything, be greater than one in four. What this identified was that the larger congregations that churches enjoy at Harvest are genuinely boosted by people attending who come only rarely. It isn't simply the bunching effect that might be produced by a higher than normal proportion of those who come often but not every Sunday all turning up on the same day.

It was the later cathedral survey in Worcester and Lichfield that gave the strongest understanding of those who were choosing primarily to express their Christian belonging through attendance at a single event. Out of 1151 people who completed the survey at the two cathedrals, 460, or around 40 per cent, indicated that they attended church five times a year or fewer. It is these that I went on to examine in more detail, and will look at further in the remainder of this chapter, as the best example of a group of people whose primary Christian belonging is likely to be through one-off events. Whilst the focus in the survey was clearly on Christmas, it becomes possible to extrapolate a wider picture of the sort of person who comes to church occasionally. And most of those who do will probably include Christmas as an important time to attend.

Even demographically, this was not a typical group of churchgoers. Among the cathedral carol service occasional attendees, the ratio of men to women was 4:5, which is noticeably more men than you find in a typical church congregation. Also, by comparison with most surveys of churchgoers, they included a much higher proportion of younger people. Some 30 per cent were below the age of 40, around 40 per cent were in the 40 to 59 range, and just fewer than 30 per cent were older.

Notwithstanding the low levels of current churchgoing, many of them were people with a significant Christian background. Four out of every five had been baptised, and over half of those baptised had also been confirmed; most of them (their ages would suggest) in an era when confirmation as an expected teenage rite of passage had died out. This confirmation figure would imply that quite a high proportion of them were people who had had some significant pattern of churchgoing at a point in the past. Academic research often refers to this group as 'church leavers'. This categorisation was borne out by the answer to another question; three-fifths agreed with the statement, *'I go to church less often nowadays.'* A few were potentially on a return path, with eight per cent agreeing with the opposite statement that they now go to church more often.

About a quarter claimed to pray at least once a week, but virtually none (no more than seven individuals) said that they read the Bible weekly or more. Despite the low levels of churchgoing, a little over half defined themselves as Church of England and a further twelve per cent as a member of another Christian denomination, almost two-thirds in total. Nearly one in five claimed to belong to the cathedral congregation itself.

There was a good level of familiarity with the concept of a carol service, with 70 per cent claiming to attend one somewhere most years and almost half claiming to do so in that cathedral.

Cathedral carol services are noted for the very high level of choral performance; so it wasn't surprising that almost everybody cited the music as one of their reasons for attending. Equally to be expected was that three-quarters agreed they were present to be reminded of the Christmas story. More encouraging were the answers to three statements that explicitly sought to tease out the presence of more religious or spiritual motivations. Majorities agreed that, *'I have come to feel close to God', 'I've come to worship God'* and, *'I've come to find the true meaning of Christmas.'* It was a slightly more general question with an implicit spiritual element, however, that gained the highest level of support, with 94 per cent agreeing that the service *'should be uplifting'*.

Taken together, the responses to these questions suggest that the finding of meaning, the possibility of encounter and the significance of public worship are important concepts within the faith of many occasional churchgoers.

There was a strong feeling that carol services should remain traditional. The two statements: *'I prefer traditional hymns to modern ones'* and *'I prefer carol services to be candlelit'* gained significantly higher levels of assent than did two that invited support for a modern idiom. At the same time, less than half expressed a preference for the use of modern English in carol services and very few agreed that they preferred modern carols to traditional ones. But might this be just a general feeling of nostalgia, a harking back to a time when these occasional churchgoers had been more involved in church life? That probably wasn't the case, since only one in twelve agreed with the statement, *'Carol services are not as good as they used to be.'* Rather, it seems that occasional carol service attendees, even though they are relatively young by comparison with most church congregations, don't have a desire to see church worship adopting overtly modern styles.

Ask enough questions and you will get some examples of what at first appear to be conflicting answers. Three-quarters agreed that, *'I like carol services that get the congregation involved'*, while little more than a third affirmed that, *'I like carol services that make me ask questions of myself.'* Taken together with the previous statements, however, I'd be inclined to suggest that this is telling us that occasional churchgoers are not merely seeking to be passive recipients of entertainment. They want to be engaged in the occasion, and to be engaged at a level that is better described as 'opening up to being affected by the experience', rather than being challenged over their theological or other beliefs.

So, what did they believe? Several statements sought out responses to elements of the Christmas story. Levels of support were highly consistent, with belief in the stable, shepherds and wise men being all a little over the halfway mark. Given that these people admit to not reading the Bible, it is not surprising that there was no significant difference between belief in these elements and the entirely non-biblical donkey. However, a second set of belief statements that more obviously required respondents to consider the possible theological import of their answers received levels of agreement well below the halfway point. Just over two in five said they believed in the virgin birth, about the same number as those who agreed that the Bible predicted Jesus' birth. Invited to consider the statement that the biblical account is not literally true, almost half assented, while over three-fifths agreed that the Christmas mystery is more important than the historical facts.

These responses build up a consistent picture of a group of people who want to enter into the Christmas story, rather than to assent to any particular theological import. I would see this not as a refusal to engage with the story as a matter of significance in their lives. What it does is express a clear preference. Occasional churchgoers at the carol service put more weight on the mystery than the history.

The light touch stance they took with regard to scripture came across even more clearly in their responses to statements about Christian beliefs: the more specific a belief, the less likely was it that they agreed with it. So while two-thirds agreed that, 'I consider myself a Christian', this dropped to a little over half who agreed that, 'I believe in God'. The level of agreement fell to two-fifths for the belief that Jesus was 'fully human', less than a third for the statement that he was 'fully God', while fewer than a quarter agreed that he was 'fully God and fully human'. The numbers make clear that some didn't agree with any of these last three statements. Consistent with the negligible level of Bible reading reported, the lowest figures for Christian belief came in the responses to statements focused on the literal truth of scripture: less than a quarter agreed that Jesus turned water into wine, one in seven that God made the world in six days and rested on the seventh, one in 20 that the Bible is without error. With this attitude to doctrine, it is not surprising that very few believed Christianity to be the only true religion and a majority believed that Christians should not try to convert people. And almost half agreed that, 'all world faiths lead to God'.

When offered the statement that, *'what you believe matters less than how you live your life'*, nearly three in five agreed; meanwhile, almost three-quarters of the sample claimed to give to charity most Christmases. Compared with the relatively low significance placed on doctrine, the answers to these two questions suggest that they consider the ethical dimension to faith to outrank the doctrinal. But is that ethical framework defined by official church teaching? The answers to two further questions would suggest that the wider moral climate holds rather greater sway. Invited to agree that it should be possible for a gay man to be made a bishop and that homosexual couples should be allowed to marry, there was support around or above the halfway mark in both cases. If anything, the slightly higher figure of support for a gay man as a bishop than for same-sex marriages indicated that the participants did not see the Church as exempt from the normal ethical standards of society.

The final area of questioning explored the attitudes of the sample to the visibility and public face of religion. This has been contested in Britain in recent years with challenges from secularist organisations and atheists on topics ranging from church schools, through prayers at council meetings, to the very use of the word 'Christmas' to describe a public holiday.

Notwithstanding the strongly pluralist view taken by participants, when asked directly whether *'Christianity should have a special place in this country'*, almost two-thirds agreed. Nearly three-fifths agreed with the principle of church schools, while only a third thought that *'Christianity and politics don't mix'*. Faith clearly has a place in the public realm for most of these individuals. Once attention was turned to Christmas itself, the responses became overwhelming; only one per cent thought that Christmas should not be a public holiday and just six per cent believed that all shops should be allowed to open on Christmas Day.

So, what have we found out about these people whose belonging with both God and the Church is primarily mediated through one-off events?

I believe that we have managed to construct a picture of what the Christian faith looks like among a population cut adrift from the ties and influences of regular churchgoing. We've turned the spotlight on to those who attend church at Christmas at a type of service that is still extremely well attended, from village church to cathedral. Rather than faith collapsing into a combination of sentiment, culture and aesthetics, I think we've seen that it retains for many a significant religious content from which can be constructed a picture of the faith of the participants.

Within this faith, a high expectation is placed on the possibility of encounter with God through participation in the style of worship offered at a carol service, and the high return rate to the service suggests that their past experience supports that expectation. The attraction and positive experience of carol service worship may owe much to the fact that the Christmas story is heard there as a narrative gateway to the mystery of God, rather than as coded doctrine. It would seem that there is a real intention on the part of the occasional churchgoers present to enter through that gateway, rather than passively to observe what is going on beyond it.

The faith engendered and supported by this encounter has been shown to be centred on doing rather than dogma. However, this is not a theology of a privatised religion; indeed, levels of private piety were quite low and Bible reading almost non-existent. Moreover, the consequence of a strong belief in pluralism is not the ejection of religion from the public realm, but a clear view that faith is a public phenomenon with a right to its place in public life, and that society needs to acknowledge it in the ordering of business, politics and education. At the same time, the values of wider society are clearly visible in the attitudes of the majority of the sample when reflecting on matters of church order. The arrow of influence in their understanding of public religion goes both ways.

If we can understand those who come occasionally to church, that will enable those planning worship, whether it be carol services or any other one-off event, including weddings and baptisms, to consider the needs and expectations of the occasional churchgoers who are likely to attend them. That is not equivalent to saying that their wishes and desires must be pandered to. Understanding is the proper precursor both to affirmation and to challenge!

Questions

- What are the key events in my life that have brought me closer to God?

- How do I feel about people who turn up at church on odd occasions?

- Do I prefer special events to be as close to Sunday worship as possible, or different, and why?

- What sort of events should be allowed to take place in church?

Chapter 5

Location, location: belonging through place

One Wednesday morning in June 2013, I was walking with my wife along Portland Street in central Manchester. We were on our way to the public announcement that I had been nominated to be the next Bishop of Manchester. Suddenly, my mind flashed back to the 1000 and more days when, as a boy, I had taken exactly that same route on my way to school. That was the moment when it really hit home to me that I had been offered an amazing opportunity to spend what might be the longest period in my ordained ministry giving something back to the place that had itself given me my start in life. I had been invited not simply to any place, but to one that had huge significance in my personal journey. Places matter. It still seems strange to drive past the house I was brought up in and to know that it no longer belongs to my family. I can't now just go to the door, turn my key and enter, in the way that I could for almost half a century. It was deeply moving to be invited back to take part in the centenary celebrations of the primary school I attended, and to lead worship in the church where I was a member of the youth group.

The day of my enthronement as Bishop of Manchester began for me in the churchyard where my grandparents are buried. Alone, I moved round the outside of the church to the place where my parents' ashes are interred. Then, joining a small congregation inside the building, I affirmed the vows made on my behalf by my godparents at the font where I was baptised, and then received Holy Communion at the place where my ancestors have done so for over a century. Only then did I feel ready to travel, on foot and by tram, to the waiting cathedral.

Places carry our memories; churches in particular carry the remembrance of our relationship with God. The celebration of the Eucharist, which stands solidly at the heart of 2000 years of Christian worship, is an act of remembering. 'Do this, as often as you eat/drink it, in remembrance of me,' says Jesus. And we do so, most of us believing that this act of remembrance creates a new situation here and now in the present. It is not simply our mental journey into the past, but Christ becoming present in a powerful and distinctive way in our midst.

Place belonging may be associated with a physical location, such as a hilltop or the site of a grave. Or it may be focused on a building, or part of it; maybe a side chapel or monument. Or it may centre upon part of the interior furnishings, perhaps the pew where I sat many years ago with a now-deceased relative. Disturbing somebody's associations with a place, even if they themselves are not consciously aware of them, is a trap that many clergy, including me, have fallen into.

As a young Team Vicar, I was determined to have removed from one of our churches a screen separating the nave from the chancel. It had been erected just after World War I, in memory of a prominent local family. It had no great antiquity in a church that had stood on the spot since medieval times; to my view, it had little of artistic merit either. It was a piece of its time, reflecting a theology of the gap between priest and laity that I found more than a little uncomfortable. Moreover, whether I was on the clergy or congregation side of it, it always made me feel as though I was watching what was happening in the other half of the church on a TV screen. I couldn't see how it could be anything other than a distraction to many others too.

It seemed that I was far from alone in my view. Experts from the diocese came out to look it over and agreed that they would welcome an application to have it removed from its current position of prominence and relocated to the side of the church towards the rear. That way it would not be lost to those who liked it as a piece of woodwork, but it would no longer be interposed between priest and congregation. At first the church council seemed minded to agree. Then one older and very longstanding member of the church let it be quietly known among her friends that the names it commemorated were members of her own family, who she remembered from childhood days. This item of furniture would be relocated over her dead body. The PCC backed off. I've no idea if the screen stands there still to this day.

Had I been aware of the difficulties that the proposal would have brought I might still have tried to achieve the same result, but at least I would have gone into the situation sensitive to the likely opposition, and sought to head it off or find a better compromise. Or I may have come to the view that it was just one of those battles that are either unwinnable or not worth winning; battles that I've spent many years as a bishop advising clergy against fighting. In either case, I would have been making an informed decision rather than a naïve one. What I had completely failed to find out was exactly what role the screen played in her sense of belonging, in that particular church, with God.

At its lowest it could simply have been that the screen itself was not so important but its removal or relegation to a less prominent position would have been highly symbolic. Was it simply about the respect that she felt her family were owed for their past significance in the parish? Was it that combined with a feeling, especially as she got older, that its relocation would have symbolised that she and those like her were themselves now being steadily relegated to the margins of the community? If so, to have it visible, but in a clearly demoted position, may have been more painful than having it simply gone from the church. Any of that would have been a sign that her relationship to the screen was about her standing within a wider community that occupied the same physical space but was very different from the one she had grown up in. It would have indicated that this was primarily a pastoral concern and we could have searched to see if an appropriate pastoral response could be found; one that would allow the church to move the screen and produce a building better fit for a modern style of worship with a greater emphasis on participation.

But was it actually a more spiritual issue? Perhaps one of those commemorated on the screen as its donors had played a crucial role in her own childhood journey to faith. Was this somebody who had first taught her to pray, or had sat with her in the family pew? Had this person introduced her to God, and had the screen erected in their memory somehow become necessary in order for her to continue to feel close to God in the same way that she had down the intervening six decades? If any of this was the case, then an agreed way forward would have had to have found some way of transferring the role played by the screen perhaps onto some other object in the church that had family connections; or maybe by creating some new memorial in its place. These may have been questions to which even she didn't have the answers, but in the event they were never even asked.

Human beings are always more complex than we imagine, and I suspect that the truth was a bit of both, a combination of family identity and pride but mixed in with a real spiritual element; the sort of connection that would have made it impossible to resolve peacefully, except through our backing off.

Perhaps it's natural that it's as I've got older and have laid down a greater stock of my own memories that the importance of place in Christian belonging has become both stronger and more evident to me. But some of it is born of listening, in my years as a bishop, to arguments in parishes over the reordering of buildings. So by the time I came to writing my 2007 Harvest survey, I was pretty clear that place was an important part of the model for belonging that I wanted to explore. How significant or not would it be, especially to congregations that contained a high proportion of people who were not frequent churchgoers?

The place-based element clearly came out for many people as a less significant factor than the people dimension. When asked to comment on the statement, *'The people here are more important to me than the place'*, over half agreed whereas only one in ten disagreed; others couldn't, or chose not to, decide. Nevertheless, if even ten per cent of churchgoers are more attracted to the building than to their fellow Christians, this says something important about the relevance that place plays. Other statements in the survey that were less forcing a choice gained significantly larger responses in favour of the role of place. Half agreed that, *'I have a strong sense of belonging to this church building'*, with only one in eight disagreeing. Over two-thirds assented to the statement, *'This church building is special to me'*, the same figure as for those who felt that, *'In this church I feel close to God.'* Finally, at just over 30 per cent, there were equal levels of agreement and disagreement with the phrase, *'It wouldn't be the same to attend a service in another church.'* When I looked at the data more deeply, I found that five out of every six people surveyed either agreed with at least one of the statements about the building, or disagreed that the people were more important. Place was evidently an important, if not the primary, aspect for the vast majority of churchgoers who completed the survey.

Place belonging does of course bring with it huge benefits for the church. It underpins the success of so many restoration appeals, where the wider community will go to enormous efforts to help the local church raise funds to complete necessary repairs. Very many major works to church buildings would not be possible without such generosity, including in my own former parishes. In one parish where I served as priest, a relatively minor act of vandalism to a stained-glass window resulted in a visit from some representatives of the community, offering to discover who had done it and to break their legs for me. The underlying sentiment was much appreciated but the offer rejected. Many parish churches remain the focal point of the community. Because, as we have noticed earlier, events are important, people want the church building to be there for their weddings and funerals and for the baptism of their descendants. But they also want it to be there to be a visible symbol that the town or village has a spiritual element to its life, and as part of its identity as a community.

All of this goes some way to explaining the difficulties faced when it is no longer possible to sustain Christian worship in every church building in an area at a prime mid-Sunday morning slot every week. It answers the questions as to why it is that country dwellers who have become quite accustomed to having to travel outside of their village to access shops, employment, leisure, medical services, schooling and for almost every other social engagement, baulk at travelling a mile down the road to join the church in the next village. This is often despite the fact that the two parishes may have shared a vicar for the last 20 years. It explains why a number of inner-city congregations contain a high proportion of worshippers who do not live in the parish and are not attracted to take any part in serving its needs during the week. They attend worship there because that is the part of town their family came from before they became wealthy enough to move out. Such churches are often burdened by the building having been constructed to accommodate the inhabitants of tightly packed Victorian industrial slums that have long been replaced by much lower density housing serving a multifaith community. When they no longer have either a congregation able to maintain them, or a strong connection that inspires the wider community to step in to help, and closure becomes inevitable, a sizable proportion of the final congregation may simply cease to go to church.

Being sensitive to the role of place doesn't turn difficult decisions into easy ones, nor does it make the impossible feasible, but it does allow for better-informed decisions, and for better pastoral and spiritual care.

Questions

- Are there places that are special in my relationship with God, and what makes them so?

- Is there anything special about the place where I worship most often now?

- How does it feel when I go into a church that is unfamiliar to me?

- Are old churches disposed of too readily?

Chapter 6

The mystery of the missing vicar: an example of belonging

The final chapter in this section is a bit of a worked example. Its focus is on the Practice of Communion by Extension, something that, with the reduced numbers of stipendiary clergy available, has become a particularly contentious and topical issue in parishes across the Church of England. I think it shows how an understanding of the different ways that people belong can shed light on a complex issue that has implications for pastoral care, public worship and our wider understanding of the nature of the Church. Even if it isn't a subject that is immediately relevant to your own church, I hope you'll find that it sparks off connections with other issues that perhaps are. Let me introduce you to it.

For at least the last 50 years, two opposing trends have been at work in the Church of England. On the one hand, it has become the prevalent view, at least outside of more evangelical circles, that the main act of public worship on Sunday morning should be sacramental. On the other hand, this same period has seen a relentless reduction in the number of stipendiary priests available to preside at Eucharists. It has become a particular issue for rural parishes, where the same vicar is shared by a number of churches. Even if there is a self-supporting priest or retired clergyperson around, there are unlikely to be enough of them for every church to have a communion service every week, even with some delicate negotiations around service times. One particular response to this was the increased usage of bread and wine that had been consecrated at some previous service, with the worship in church then being led by a Reader or some other authorised layperson.

Like many practices in the Church of England, it had grown up steadily, the idea passing from parish to parish, as a practical solution to a practical problem. I'd met it myself, very early in my ordained ministry. The vicar was going on holiday, leaving me, a deacon of some three weeks' experience, to get on with things in his absence. He had made arrangements for visiting priests to come in and lead the main service each week whilst he was away. Now, only a few days before his departure, one of them rang to cancel. He did his best to find another priest, one who just happened to have a free Sunday at the start of the school summer holidays and at only a few days' notice but, to no great surprise, it proved impossible. It was too late to announce a change from Holy Communion to Morning Prayer, so he simply consecrated enough bread and wine to cover a normal Sunday, locked it in the aumbry, and told me to take the service as normal; just leave out the Eucharistic Prayer. Everything passed off fine. Indeed, I quite enjoyed having the congregation to myself.

Three or so years later, in a Team Ministry with three churches and just one other priest and a newly ordained deacon, it was no longer an emergency procedure. Each church had communion from the reserved sacrament one week in three. At this period the Church of England was also beginning to ordain women as deacons, but not yet as priests. Some of them were very experienced and rapidly became appointed as 'Deacon in Charge' to a parish which might then have no resident priest serving it. Bringing in a male priest, largely to say the Eucharistic Prayer, each week was not only laborious in such circumstances but also seemed to fly in the face of the role of the woman who was, as far as most parishioners could see, in all other aspects their vicar. Again, to have the sacrament previously consecrated seemed a natural solution.

Things were probably allowed to continue to develop, somewhat under the radar, because the Church of England had, even by then, a long history of struggling to make any headway on formal provision, either for the use of the reserved sacrament in church or the taking of Holy Communion after a service to the sick. Neither of these practices presented any theological difficulty to Anglo-Catholic or Central

Anglicans, but to those of a more evangelical or Protestant bent, they reopened controversies from the Reformation era. Did the consecrated bread and wine retain a status that allowed them to be used for later communion? And was it possible to allow for them to be set aside for such purposes without being seen to have given back door approval to practices of eucharistic adoration that appeared at loggerheads with the 39 Articles of Religion of the Church?

Caught between the practical developments in parishes across the country and objections rooted in differences over sacramental theology, it took until 2000 before the General Synod got round to authorising a rite for what became known as Communion by Extension. The next year the House of Bishops produced a set of guidelines to accompany it. The aim was to allow some leeway for what was already happening, whilst trying to set some firm limits as to when it was appropriate. It's worth quoting the key paragraph from what the bishops wrote.

> In making authorized provision for Communion by Extension, the House of Bishops has in mind the needs of a single cure with a number of authorised places of worship, or a group or team ministry. In such circumstances worshippers gathered in one of the places where Holy Communion has not been celebrated may receive communion by extension from a church where Holy Communion is celebrated, with a minimal interval of time between the services. The provision is intended primarily for Sundays and Principal Holy Days, but may be appropriate on other occasions. A particular congregation should not come to rely mainly upon this means of Eucharistic participation, and care should be taken to ensure that a celebration of Holy Communion takes place regularly in each church concerned.[5]

The rites themselves contain material to be spoken out loud by the person leading worship that refer explicitly to the link between the service taking place and the one at which, earlier the same day, the elements had been consecrated. The central notion is not that the life of the consecrated elements is being extended, but rather it is the altar rail that is being extended beyond the building in which the first congregation has gathered. It now stretches to another group of worshippers elsewhere in the same benefice, in the same way that it might previously have been extended to encompass the sickbed of a church member. While there is no explicit statement that the service is not to be used for reasons such as holiday cover, sickness and vacancies, or for managing the general workload of the priest, the phrasing makes it clear that these latter circumstances should be much rarer occurrences. The fact that the rite did not have an easy journey through the synodical process might have been a strong hint that it was also going to encounter problems in practice.

So what did happen? Four years later, noticing a growth in the number of applications, I thought it worth setting aside some time to see what was going on in the diocese of Worcester, where by then I was Bishop of Dudley. I found that in the period from January 2004 to August 2005, some 22 applications for permission, or substantial items of correspondence relating to Communion by Extension, had come in to the bishop's office. Between them they covered about a fifth of the churches in the diocese. Whilst three of these fell fully within the guidelines, the others breached them in a variety of ways. Some of these departures from the House of Bishops' intentions suggested that the theological assumptions of the guidelines were being contravened.

Almost every one of the guidelines was breached in at least one of the applications. Some were clearly directed towards staffing regular midweek Eucharists, particularly during holiday periods or vacancies. Another group reflected a reluctance to ask already very busy clergy from neighbouring parishes to come and help them out. A third group were looking to use the provision for early morning Eucharists, ahead of a main Sunday Communion service in the same church. They cited the difficulty of getting cover from retired clergy at such an early hour of the day. Others made it clear that they intended to store the consecrated elements from at least the previous Sunday, if not even earlier.

The reasons given were primarily practical. But they began to set out a clear example of how all the four dimensions of the model of Christian belonging that we have been looking at come into play around a single topic.

Belonging through activities

Having the same service, at the same time and place, is of huge importance to our sense of belonging through regular activity. This isn't just true for the main Sunday morning congregation, but equally for the other occasions on which churchgoers gather for worship. Early morning services may have fewer people in attendance, but for those who are there, they matter enormously. Midweek services have increasingly developed a life of their own over recent years. They are no longer a service for the most devout and least busy to come along to in addition to Sunday attendance. In many parishes there are significant, if not large, numbers of churchgoers for whom the midweek service is their primary or only engagement with public worship.

Some of the reasons for this are not hard to uncover. Public transport on Sunday mornings can be difficult to find, even in the most densely populated areas. Many worshippers are reluctant to be part of a formal scheme for providing them with lifts to and from church. Such arrangements are perceived as constraining; they take away that ability to make a last-minute decision as to whether to go or not on any particular occasion. Such independence is something that has become a much valued assertion of autonomy in many people's lives. If anything, this freedom becomes even more important to people who feel that their independence is being constrained in other ways, such as declining health.

In some cases the midweek or early morning service has become the remaining option for those who prefer communion in traditional language, and usually according to the Book of Common Prayer. For people who have said and heard those same familiar words from their first childhood experiences of churchgoing, the vocabulary has itself become an essential part of the activity that brings them close to God. One church I visited held a weekly Monday morning Eucharist at eleven o'clock to which were brought about 15 people who would normally at that time be attending a centre for adults with dementia conditions. About an equal number of other members of the church were present. It was extremely moving to see and hear people who for most of the time appeared only vaguely aware of what was going on around them come alive as they joined in the traditional words of the service and then as they received the sacrament. More modern words would not have done. It needed to be the language that took them back to much earlier times and awakened memories and links. Much of what else happened to them during the week may well have been confusing or vague, but for that brief moment they were as fully engaged in worship as anyone.

Others have a pattern of working or family commitments that makes regular mid-morning Sunday worship difficult to sustain, but other times of the week are less pressured. Family may have to be visited or grandchildren cared for. Shift patterns may require frequent weekend working, or a child may have a regular sporting commitment for which they require transport. Rather than come sometimes to the main service and at other times earlier or midweek, an individual may prefer the routine of regular midweek or early worship. In one parish where I was Team Rector, the main employment was agricultural. If Sunday dawned bright and fair, then the morning might have to be spent on the farm. Over a period of several years, a Thursday evening Eucharist grew until it was almost as well frequented as Sunday morning.

One other and rather distinct aspect of Communion by Extension arose in terms of the people who frequently led it. I questioned one incumbent who had a midweek service at a time when he had a regular other commitment. It would have been easily possible to move the service a little earlier or later, so that on most occasions he would be there to take it. In reply he told me that the two people who regularly led this worship had become very attached to the role of doing so.

Whilst the congregation might accept a move to a different time, these particular individuals would feel that something which had become an important, even central, part of their own relationship with God, had been torn from them. It mattered to them that they led this service, and that they did so on a regular and frequent basis. It had become one of their core 'activities'. That something has become part of how someone belongs doesn't of course make it a trump card that should be guaranteed to win against any challenge. There are plenty of situations in churches—for example, an officer who has held a particular role for too long—when the price of the well-being of the whole church has to be an unwelcome change for an individual or group within the congregation. But in all these situations, to understand how a particular activity has taken on a key role in a person's sense of belonging, even their belonging with God, is to at least enter the fray less unprepared.

Most parishes do not set up such services unless there is an expectation that on a large majority of occasions there will be an ordained member of the local church available to lead it. Communion by Extension allows the regularity to be guaranteed. The service will not be cancelled because the vicar has got to take a funeral, nor will it be changed to an unfamiliar (and to those for whom the regularity of the activity is a key factor, unwelcome) liturgy such as Morning Prayer or a Service of the Word. It won't be suspended during clergy holidays nor entirely abandoned during a vacancy. Other options, such as finding a priest from elsewhere, are of course available, but we will go on to look at why they are equally unpopular for many in the following sections of this chapter.

Belonging through people

Having read the correspondence received by the diocese, I arranged a couple of lunches where I could speak with clergy and laypeople from parishes that had held services of Communion by Extension, and to prepare for them I emailed out a short list of questions that might cover the topics we would discuss over our meal. What began to emerge, and rather to my surprise, was a strong sense of how it was 'people belonging' factors that were perhaps the prime driver behind many requests.

One of the questions I asked was why some of these parishes did not try to invite retired clergy to preside at Eucharists, especially at main Sunday services. We were a diocese into which many clergy moved at the point of retirement, especially into the market towns that dotted the more rural south. Some deaneries had many more active retired clergy than they did licensed stipendiary and self-supporting ministers put together.

Initial responses focused on practical factors. I was told that a visiting priest would have to be paid travel expenses, and might even want to charge them a £10 fee for taking the service. Then it was said that the task of having to ring round several retired clergy until one was found who was available would place an unnecessary additional administrative burden on whoever had to do it. None of this really seemed like sufficient reason to embark upon an entirely new form of public worship, and it soon became clear that these were only a cover for much deeper, and in some cases perhaps subconscious, issues. What emerged as our conversations went on was that the prime reason for choosing Communion by Extension over finding a priest from elsewhere was so that the worship would be led by 'one of our own'.

I pressed it a little bit further. It was obvious that parishes which were opting for these services had home-grown leaders, usually Readers, who they felt were competent to lead. Would it not be a better arrangement for the local leadership to lead most of the service, including preaching the sermon, but to have a visitor do those things that must be led by an ordained priest? Even here they were adamant. It would still be a visitor presiding over their act of worship, and that wasn't what they wanted. They identified with their own vicar and with other clergy licensed or with permission to officiate who they considered as members of their parish. They didn't identify with a priest from outside. He or she was not somebody who would adequately mediate their sense of belonging to God through the Eucharist in the same way as would an appropriately qualified layperson drawn from among their own congregation.

It wasn't about the quality of worship that a visitor might offer. It wasn't even that with an outsider that quality would be unknown. It was simply a strong sense that in this act of worship that most powerfully expresses our belonging with God, it matters that the person leading is one with whom we already have a clear sense of belonging.

The theological positions which people reach, not as a result of formal teaching and education, but simply through their experience of engaging with God as part of his Church, form an area of study known as 'Ordinary Theology'. It's a topic that has fascinated me for some years. What I was hearing was an excellent case study in it. The official church position might well be that when the priest presides at the Eucharist, especially when they do so facing the congregation, she or he is standing in the place of Christ. It might well be that the wearing of robes by the president, as required by Canon Law, serves to further underline that the personality and individual identity of the priest is of little consideration. But none of this stands a chance in the face of men and women reflecting on their own experience of what draws them closer to God.

One or two of the applications came from a different perspective. Some parishes had discovered that the services to which they were attracting new members were non-eucharistic. All-age worship in particular was reaching out to younger families and individuals in the community. In some cases these services had begun less as a call to outreach and more as a mechanism for allowing the priest to be presiding at Eucharists elsewhere, in a complex monthly worship rota. God had blessed them and they were now the cutting edge of the parish's mission. Unfortunately, the service pattern meant that those who were being reached by them, but not attending Eucharists, never met the vicar. In order that they should be able to do so, and to develop a sense of belonging with their parish priest that might strengthen their religious belonging, the request was to allow Communion by Extension to be used to free up the vicar to be a more visible lead and presence at these occasions. Notwithstanding that such missional imperatives had not noticeably formed any part of the thinking of the General Synod or House of Bishops in framing the guidelines, these seemed like some of the most important ventures to encourage and support.

Belonging through events and place

In one parish where I was incumbent we had two churches, about three miles apart. The larger had a tradition of a Christmas Eve Midnight Mass, the other, at the less populated end of the patch, didn't. A few people from that congregation would join the larger church for their service. One year I was approached by an occasional churchgoer who asked whether it would be possible to have a midnight service in the other church. They had taken some soundings around the village and felt that a decent number of people might want to come. It seemed worth a try, and that year we had two ordained priests available, so we did it. The church was packed.

Christmas midnight worship is clearly an event. It happens just once a year, and unlike many other annual or occasional events, the Eucharist is an essential part of it. And for those who were only occasional churchgoers, it mattered that it was taking place within the church building with which they had a sense of belonging. The church in the other half of the parish, even if the worship was led by me and attended by a number of people who went to their own church, would not be the same.

A small number of the applications for Communion by Extension had Christmas particularly in mind. They came from rural benefices where a sole vicar normally spent Sunday mornings taking Holy Communion in different churches at staggered times. It wasn't possible to arrange midnight services at such varied intervals; the practice of having a mid-evening Eucharist on Christmas Eve may work in many Roman Catholic parishes but has never caught on among Anglicans. Midnight means the worship has to straddle that specific time. One benefice had done its homework carefully. They felt it was important that the sacrament consumed in each church should have been freshly consecrated at a Christmas service in the benefice. They had held practice runs to time how long it would take to transport the bread and wine from the most geographically suitable church to the others. A slight variation in starting times in each church would allow a fast car to take the elements that the vicar had just consecrated to each other church just in time for them to be shared in a service led by a layperson. It worked perfectly.

Communion by Extension and belonging

The practice of Communion by Extension, as it was growing in the Church of England both before and after the General Synod spent time and energy considering it, has taken little notice of either official guidelines or formal theological understandings. It has developed rather as a means to sustain belonging in each of the four dimensions that this book is seeking to explore. Looking at it has proved useful to us as a worked example of how engaging with the ways in which people belong can shed light onto church practices that have grown up relatively unexamined. It doesn't provide an easy solution to complex pastoral problems, but it allows an informed rather than naïve response to be made to them.

At the same time, it raises challenges to some basic aspects of Anglican understanding of the Church. Where such a high importance is placed on people and places that are very local to us, how do we guard against an unwitting congregationalism, one where the local gathered church enjoys its self-sufficiency and has little sense of belonging to anything outside its parish boundaries? Indeed, is such a congregationalism already widespread, signalled often by the reluctance of some churches to pay any more in parish share than they themselves get back directly?

My beginnings of an answer to that question would lie in developing an understanding of the place of the priest as not simply the local leader of the church but its link to something beyond itself. And of the bishop as a visible human sign and a call to espouse a belonging that is not complete without a sense of being part of something greater, both in time and space. The local church is only the Church when it is visibly linked to the universal Church.

Questions

- Do I find it easier to worship when the leader is somebody I know?

- To what extent do I feel that I belong to a church that is wider than my own congregation or parish?

- Does it matter if I take Easter communion from elements consecrated during Lent?

- Should suitable lay people from the local church be authorised to preside at Communion services there?

Part
Two

Belonging for mission

Introduction

The first part of this book has set out a model of the variety of ways in which people belong with God through the Christian, and more specifically Church of England, Church. I hope it's done enough to show that Christian belonging cannot simply be collapsed into the things that people commit themselves to doing, publicly or privately, on a regular basis. For those of us who are at the heart of organised religious life, it will continue to be committed activities that play a high role in what draws us to practise, sustain and develop our faith. But we live in an age and culture in which, whilst notions such as 'spirituality', a sense of life beyond the material and even explicit assent to belief in God and Jesus Christ, remain prevalent, commitment to regular participant membership of all organisations, including religious ones, fights an uphill battle. In many ways it can be argued that regular active churchgoing has contracted more slowly through the last century than have most other secular expressions of belonging. The decline in active participant membership of clubs and societies, including trade unions, adult educational institutes, the many local philanthropic and social organisations for men, and others, has been more rapid. For many of us, membership is characterised by the National Trust subscription. We join as a sign of general support for the aims of the organisation. We are happy to part with a modest financial contribution towards its work and are glad to be able to visit its properties once in a while when the urge takes us. We may even purchase modest mementoes of our visits to take home or give to our friends. But only a few of us aspire to be regular volunteers.

What I've sought to suggest is that the three other dimensions of belonging demonstrate a much wider, if less tangible, religious identity. Yet it is one that is increasingly important for churches to understand and engage with if we are to fulfil our vocation under God. The second part of this book will focus on how we work with the grain of this wider religious identity. We will need to build on what we discovered earlier about those who come to the cathedral carol service, in order to develop a clearer understanding of people who belong primarily through people, places and events. What do they believe about God? How do they engage with the society around them?

The two surveys that I carried out as part of the research that led to this book have one obvious limitation. They both relied on people coming to church to fill in their responses. Other researchers have found clear evidence of numbers of people who retain a strong sense of Christian identity and belonging but who have ceased to take any part in public worship. But the objective of my writing is not to set out a comprehensive description of all Christian identity. My aim is to apply my research findings to help local churches engage with those most close to them; those who are relatively easy to reach and yet to whom the church struggles to pay adequate attention.

Our task among such people is, I believe, twofold. It includes our desire to find ways of encouraging them to engage more frequently and more deeply with the organised life of the church, in the strong belief that this is the best way to grow and mature in faith. Put bluntly, I want to see church congregation numbers growing through the drawing in of those who have up to this point in time been only occasionally present in our pews or seats. But the second part of our task is to recognise that for some, a true Christian belonging will never express itself in frequent churchgoing. This isn't a proof of apathy; it just reflects the way they belong to anything. We are called to be a priestly people, serving not just our congregations but the spiritual needs of the community as a whole. As a sign of this, every licensed parish priest is given a share in the bishop's 'cure of souls' that extends to the whole population of the benefice. To help people to belong more strongly through occasional churchgoing, through the people who mediate something of God's presence in their community and through the buildings and places that resonate with God for them, is central to our calling.

The next group of chapters will explore this further.

Chapter 7

What's the difference? Understanding occasional churchgoers

My first big attempt to look at people who come to church occasionally came with my inviting 27 Worcester churches, in predominantly rural areas, to administer a survey to every adult attending their church Harvest service. Harvest is a festival with relatively little doctrinal weight to it. It's a Victorian addition to the Christian calendar. It was only invented by the Reverend Robert Stephen Hawker in the Cornish parish of Morwenstow in 1843. Yet within the space of a generation it had become part of the furniture in Church of England parishes in both villages and towns. There were several good reasons for choosing Harvest over and above a normal Sunday, or one of the other, perhaps more obvious, festivals in the Christian year. Firstly, I hoped for bigger congregations, so that the same number of churches would produce a larger volume of replies. Secondly, Harvest feels like a celebration of the local area, especially if that area is rural, so there might well be people there who had a good range of connections in the local community. Finally, and perhaps most important of all, because of its lack of link to any particular doctrinal message beyond the creation, attendance at it would not necessarily be seen as a commitment to a very specific view of religion or Christianity.

To my delight, some 1454 surveys were returned. With an average of just over 50, the number of individual responses from a church ranged from nine to 143. There was also a high rate of response to each individual question, something necessary if I wasn't going to have to discard lots of the replies.

As soon as I began to explore the data I realised that I'd got hold of a very interesting collection of people. Demographically, the people who had responded were typical of Worcestershire C of E churchgoers; two-thirds of them were women and 60 per cent were over the age of 60. What surprised me was that although the majority were reasonably regular churchgoers, once a month or more, that still left over a quarter who admitted to only coming rarely, half a dozen times a year or fewer. The Harvest service wasn't just an occasion when regular churchgoers made extra effort to get to church, it was genuinely reaching out to a wider population. In total, 326 people who only came occasionally had completed all or almost all of the survey. It looked like it might be interesting to compare and contrast these with the 775 who said they came to church nearly every week, or indeed more often. Those numbers were more than sufficient to allow proper statistical analysis to be undertaken. I primed up my computer and started to crunch numbers. The rest of this chapter sets out some of the things that emerged.

Believing in God

One of the standard questions asked in surveys of religious affiliation is to invite people to indicate their level of assent or otherwise to the simple statement, 'I believe in God.' But why ask one question when you can ask three? Maybe it would be worth seeing if a more specific statement, 'I believe in Jesus Christ', would sort between the generally religious and the specifically Christian. Working from the opposite direction, the statement, 'I believe in a higher power', might show if the Harvest service was attracting people with a more vague sense of spirituality, who would prefer to affirm a statement cast in the most vague and general terms possible, along the lines popularised by groups such as Alcoholics Anonymous. Given that many recent and 'new age' spiritualities seek a strong connection with the natural order, if these people existed and were ever going to turn up, Harvest was the best time to find them.

The results were the exact opposite of what might have been expected. Belief in Jesus gained the highest rate of assent among occasional churchgoers, with four out of five agreeing. It was just three per cent ahead of belief in God, but fewer than three in five believed in a higher power. When I worked out the figures for the regular churchgoers, the numbers agreeing were higher in every case, but the large gap between belief in God and Jesus and belief in a higher power was exactly the same. It felt like an encouraging thing to discover, that it is the person of Jesus that occasional churchgoers most want to identify with. As I said much earlier in this book, the Christian faith is a relational one. There's a very strong link between what it is to belong to the people with whom I have my most important relationships and what it is to belong to Jesus Christ. The survey results suggested that these occasional churchgoers were indeed ones for whom 'belonging through people' would be a high factor in their faith.

Believing in the Bible

One reason why people might not feel comfortable being in church regularly is a feeling that they may be expected to believe in the historical accuracy of the Bible to a degree that they are uncomfortable with. So how did they compare with their more frequent churchgoing neighbours in the Harvest pews? This time just a couple of statements were put to them for an indication of assent or otherwise.

The first statement, *'I believe Jesus really turned water into wine'*, picks up on the events of the wedding at Cana in Galilee. It's the first of Jesus' miracles told in the Gospel of St John and one of the most familiar stories in the Gospels. Part of the attraction of asking people about whether they believe this particular story to be true is that it isn't closely tied to any specific Christian doctrine, nor is it something that has been a bone of contention. People would be likely to be able to answer the question, but it would not be something they had pondered and struggled long and hard over. Finally, unlike the healing miracles, which naturally lead to discussion about whether similar healings by faith can be performed today, nature miracles such as this are more firmly rooted in a single occurrence.

There was quite a big difference found between the frequent and occasional churchgoers. Three in five of the former believed in the miracle, just over one in three of the latter did, not much more than half as many.

The second statement offered in the survey, *'I believe God made the world in six days and rested on the seventh'*, was of a very different kind. The issue of whether or not there was a six-day creation relates to a core Christian doctrine. However, the biblical account has been subjected to overwhelming scientific challenge for over a century. Much present-day Christian theology formulates its understanding of creation in a way that rejects or downplays the historicity of the account in Genesis 1–2 in favour of seeing the biblical story as an account of 'why' the world came into being rather than a scientific description of 'how' it did. Whilst much mainstream Christian belief has followed this direction and accepted some version of an evolutionary understanding of creation, for others, as witnessed by periodic disputes over the teaching of it in secondary school science lessons, assent to what is often referred to as 'creationism' has become a litmus test of Christian orthodoxy.

Here too there was some difference between how the groups responded to the statement, with the occasional churchgoers again being just over half as likely to agree with it. But the figures for agreement were very much lower in both cases. Just over a third of frequent churchgoers affirmed the six-day creation, only a fifth of the occasional ones did.

Taken together, the responses to these two statements show that occasional churchgoers sit more loosely to the literal truth of the Bible than do those who attend very often. But they tell us rather more than just that. They give a clear indication that the less literal occasional churchgoers are not turning up and finding themselves isolated among a congregation who are united behind a more conservative position.

Rather, there are many in the church sharing their positions. The figures for the regular churchgoers also suggest that literal belief in the Bible is not something that they are being taught from their pulpits. So again, those coming once in a while are unlikely to find themselves being urged to make a change in their understanding if they are to be accepted among the congregation.

Believing in Christianity

The communities of rural Worcestershire where this survey was carried out are not among the most religiously diverse in Britain; however, the towns to which people travel to access work, healthcare and many other essential services are considerably more so. It was likely that those completing the questionnaire had some basic knowledge of other faiths, but perhaps only limited direct experience of engaging in conversations about faith with those of other beliefs. Politically, the area could be described as mildly conservative. So what would they make of questions inviting them to reflect on exclusive truth claims?

Less than half of either group were ready to give assent to the statement, *'Christianity is the only true religion'*, though the regular churchgoers were significantly more likely to agree—two out of every five by contrast with under a quarter of the occasional attendees. To a similar statement, but put the other way round, *'All world faiths lead to God'*, there was not only a positive majority among both groups but the small difference between them was not statistically significant. It would seem that both regular and occasional Anglican churchgoers are predominantly pluralist in their understanding of religious truth claims. Again, there wasn't a difference that should make occasional churchgoers feel alienated.

Believing in churchgoing

Central to the thesis of this book is the notion that regular churchgoing is not the only way in which Christian belonging is expressed, and for many it appears not to be an essential way. But what did the Harvest congregations themselves think about that?

One particular statement has generated a large amount of academic study in recent times, so it felt worth including it in its most commonly used form, *'You don't have to go to church to be a good Christian.'* It wasn't surprising that the vast majority, four in every five, of those who themselves only get to church once in a while, wished to agree with the statement. More surprising was that over half of the frequent churchgoers did too. That leaves plenty of scope for asking, as this book is seeking to do, what it is other than churchgoing that might make for a 'good Christian'.

Believing in religion

There is now quite a body of research to demonstrate that belonging as defined by self-declaration, such as agreement with the statement *'I consider myself a Christian'*, is found in a significantly higher percentage of populations than belief as measured by more doctrinally focused statements. It seemed well worth putting this specific statement into the survey. But, since we were trying to tease out the positions of those who are less often in church, perhaps a couple of other questions might flesh it out. The first was intended to be a little more general: *'I consider myself a religious person.'* Then, to investigate those wary of organised religion: *'I consider myself a spiritual person.'*

As with the questions about belief in God, the ranking of the answers came out rather different than might have been expected. For both groups it was the 'Christian' statement that attracted by far the highest support. Almost all the frequent churchgoers agreed, along with five out of every six of the others. Among those who come to church very often, being 'religious' was, at four in five, ten per cent ahead of being 'spiritual'. Among the occasional churchgoers, both these statements were agreed by about half the respondents.

The relative unwillingness of both frequent and occasional churchgoers to define themselves as 'religious' as opposed to Christian is somewhat surprising. It doesn't appear from the survey to be doctrinal diffidence; the figures for self-declared belief in 'God' and in 'Jesus Christ' were more or less the same as the figure for self-defining as 'Christian'. Could it be possible that the term 'religious' was seen to carry connotations well beyond doctrinal assent? Perhaps to be 'religious' implies in some people's minds either patterns of behaviour or a degree of commitment, above and beyond frequent attendance at worship, that some baulked at allying themselves with. And perhaps the same is true, even more so, of the word 'spiritual'. Rather than allowing a wider degree of inclusion, it implies a commitment to involvement in spiritual practices, however undefined such a commitment may be left. To be Christian is perceived as more rather than less general than either of these; which, if we are right that Christian belonging is built of factors such as place, event and people as well as through regular practice, should perhaps not have been so surprising.

Believing in traditional worship

I've often heard it argued, though never with any evidence to back it up, that what churches need in order to attract people on the fringes of churchgoing to their worship are more modern-style services, probably more modern than the regular congregation itself prefers. Or, it would seem, the people who turn up for Harvest.

By majorities of three to two, both frequent and occasional churchgoers agreed that, *'I like services using traditional language'*. Support from both sides grew even higher, reaching four to one, for the statement, *'I like traditional hymns'*. Whilst there was also strong agreement with the statement, *'I like services that get the congregation involved'*, and again no statistical difference between the responses of the two groups, it was the final statement that found a distinct response. When faced with the phrase, *'I like services to be fresh and challenging'*, it was the frequent churchgoers, at 70 per cent, who were the more likely to agree.

It may be that Harvest is a particularly traditional occasion, and that the occasional churchgoers it attracts are more similar to their frequent churchgoing counterparts than might be found on other occasions, but my hunch, backed up by the findings from the survey, is that the desire for more modern styles of worship is often driven by those in leadership positions in the church, who are projecting their own aspirations on to the wider community, than it is a genuine need in that larger constituency. People who come to church once in a while are more likely to prefer to find something that hasn't changed too radically from the last time they turned up.

Picturing our churchgoers

Before we go on to reflect on the results of the survey and their implications for ministry and mission, let's just pause to briefly sketch a picture of the beliefs and attitudes of both the regular and occasional rural churchgoer.

We've found that the frequent churchgoer is a person of broad liturgical tastes. They are moderately pluralist, and accept biblical statements where they do not contradict scientific evidence. They are fairly comfortable with the description 'religious', believe in God and Jesus Christ and self-identify as Christian.

The occasional churchgoer is pluralist as regards world faiths. They do not treat the Bible as historically accurate and they regard church attendance as very much an optional extra. However, they continue to believe in God and in Jesus Christ and make a positive choice to self-identify as Christian. They are not seeking more modern or interactive styles of worship than appeal to regular churchgoers. They are not attracted by notions of spirituality.

Building on traditional words and patterns

Both groups responded more positively to traditional words such as 'God', 'Jesus Christ' and 'Christian' than they did to more vague notions of 'spirituality' and 'higher power'. There is a strong steer here that both in the task of nurturing regular congregations and in reaching out to occasional churchgoers there is little to be gained from seeking to adopt what might be seen as more inclusive terms. People respond better to the language with which they are familiar. Indeed, the survey found equally among both groups strong positive responses to the use of traditional language and traditional hymns.

The survey results suggest that the church would be advised in its teaching and preaching ministry to focus on adding to the content and meaning with which individuals fill out traditional terms rather than seeking to replace them. Preaching might be advised to emphasise the Gospel stories of Jesus, and to do so in ways that allow a congregation to identify with him.

The term 'spirituality' is now widely used in church circles. In addition to the general exposure of churchgoers to the media and bookshops, many dioceses and other bodies advertise courses on it, and many books are written for a specifically Christian readership containing the word in their titles or description. Parish profiles drawn up to attract candidates for an incumbency often refer to it either as a quality sought in their next vicar or an area in which the benefice wishes to deepen its life and experience. It is unlikely, then, that unfamiliarity with the term explains the lower levels of agreement found for it among regular churchgoers. A more plausible reason is, as suggested earlier, that it carries connotations of a depth of faith and practice that many outside of the most active church members are aware they do not experience and perhaps don't even aspire to.

In terms of helping people deepen their individual relationship with God, the survey suggests that a better strategy might be to avoid the concept of 'spirituality' and instead try to flesh out and broaden how both regular and occasional churchgoers understand more traditional terms such as 'prayer'. Rather than seeking to replace the traditional word, the challenge is to counteract the slippage by which it collapses through lack of attention into notions of 'shopping lists' rather than carrying the full weight of the Christian spiritual tradition. Other aspects of the somewhat wide term 'spirituality' may benefit from the same treatment.

The support for traditional language, and even more strongly for traditional hymns, by both groups must not be understated. When combined with the positive responses from both groups about congregational involvement and freshness, a picture can be built up that again is centred upon building on the past rather than seeking to replace it. The notion of interactive participation cuts across many facets of British society from the growth of two-way internet communications (of which Twitter is merely one of the most recent examples) via TV audiences voting for the results of competitions and on to the highly consultative processes that have featured in the production of many recent civil parish plans. Church congregations are happy to be more actively involved during public worship than perhaps was the case in previous generations because the wider culture conditions them to be so. In practice, a pattern appears to have grown up in many English parishes whereby interactive worship makes significantly less use of traditional liturgical texts and language and of traditional hymns than is the case when less participative models are used. The evidence of this survey suggests the opposite course of action would be more positively received, namely that in preparing fresh, challenging and interactive forms of worship, the use of rather more traditional material will enhance the worship experience for both occasional and regular churchgoers.

Sitting lightly to absolute truth claims and demands

It's not the purpose of this book to adjudicate between conservative and more liberal views within the Church. What I hope to achieve is to set out observations and findings that can help inform mission and ministry whatever the particular churchmanship tradition of a specific congregation or parish. Whatever our personal standpoints, if our engagement with those who don't come to church very often is to be fruitful, then it needs to be grounded in an informed understanding of both our existing congregations and those whom we are seeking to engage with.

In terms of understanding of the scriptures, it's important that we don't read too much into the response by two groups to only two statements. However, what we've seen suggests strongly that biblical literalism is a minority position among both frequent and infrequent Anglican churchgoers. Among the churches surveyed, there were one or two that I would have expected to take a clear conservative stance; believing and preaching strongly that a high view of biblical inerrancy is a necessary part of following Jesus Christ. A large amount of the support for six-day creation is likely to have come from these congregations.

Moreover, the fact that one in five occasional attendees also affirmed a six-day creation suggests that much of the support for the concept is more likely to be composed of factors beyond the teaching of the local church. There may well be some Christians who, in wanting to react strongly against the well-publicised views of atheist commentators, do so by taking a more overtly conservative view than they would otherwise adopt. But for many, it may simply be that their attitudes to creation are not the result of careful and prayerful thinking and consideration, but are relatively unexamined.

Among regular churchgoers only, the level of support for a 'minor' Gospel miracle was considerably higher than the support for six-day creation. Perhaps familiarity both with this specific narrative and with the many other accounts of Gospel miracles has an impact on the beliefs of regular churchgoers. Hearing them over and over again makes the stories seem more inherently plausible than they would be to a person less familiar with them. As with traditional language and hymns, the importance of familiarity cannot be understated. However, even here, fewer than 60 per cent felt able to affirm the statement offered. Biblical truth claims do not, for most churchgoers, and especially for occasional attendees, trump a person's everyday experience of how the world is or their awareness of specific scientific evidence that runs counter to the scriptural narrative. But neither does a willingness to doubt some Bible stories lead to a loss of faith.

The high level of support within both groups for a pluralistic attitude to religious truth adds further weight to the case that for many churchgoers, and especially occasional ones, truth claims are not taken for granted but are examined from the perspective of the wider culture and society within which an individual lives. Despite the regular occurrence of very high-profile incidents of religiously motivated violent extremism across the world, and the consequent significant negative media reporting on Islam in particular, the post-modern notion that truth is pluriform and that a wide range of inconsistent but sincerely held beliefs can be affirmed, continues to hold sway. Meanwhile, statements of exclusivity, and in particular, suggestions that other faiths are untrue or ineffective, are resisted.

Churches which place biblical historicity and exclusivist claims at the heart of their mission are faced with a major task in seeking to overturn the views of both regular church members and those who they are attracting to occasional participation. If, as suggested here, resistance to both biblical and religious truth claims are part of a general attitude, it is likely that both would need to be addressed together. There is a delicate tightrope to be walked between asserting these claims sufficiently strongly to those taking part in church activities and not at the same time discouraging those on the fringes of church life and alienating the wider community. Whilst this may be more possible in a suburban or urban setting, where the links between Church and community are often less close, the task is going to be harder in a rural setting.

For other churches, the evidence is that churchgoers are by and large comfortable with preaching and teaching that accepts the mainstream tradition of biblical criticism, engages respectfully with those of other world faiths and presents the Christian faith for positive reasons rather than through seeking to falsify the truth claims of others. In making such an appeal to those attracted to occasional participation, the church is inviting them to grow and adapt their world view rather than to discard it.

The evangelistic gap

One of the key findings of the survey that lies behind this chapter is that a majority of regular churchgoers did not take the view that attending church was necessary in order to be a 'good Christian'. The idea that the Christian faith makes an absolute demand in terms of public worship does not attract even many of those who themselves choose to attend on a weekly basis. This leaves us with something of an evangelistic dilemma for the Church of England. Members of church congregations, who are in many respects the best placed to invite and encourage their friends and neighbours into regular church attendance, are unlikely to overcome their natural reserve in doing so if they take the view that it is not at the heart of what being a Christian is about. Yet, if as I've argued, a large number of occasional churchgoers are motivated in their belonging through personal relationship, then it may be precisely just such an invitation that they are waiting for.

However, we have a model of belonging that operates in more than two dimensions. So, if the appeal cannot be simply a people-based 'Come with me to church', then it may well be more enthusiastically delivered and received if it is an event-based 'Come with me this Sunday because it's our special…' It may be that outreach strategies based on a regular series of one-off events prove more successful in some places than relational ones. Not least because they are working with rather than against the grain of the understanding of churchgoing that both regular and infrequent attendees would appear to share. The successes in some places of 'Back to Church Sunday' and the more recent notion of a 'season of invitation' may have important lessons to contribute.

Questions

- Is it true that you don't have to go to church to be a good Christian?

- If many occasional churchgoers prefer a less innovative style, what does that say about how we should appeal to them?

- Is it possible to have a heart for evangelism at the same time as believing that all world religions lead to God?

- How far should regular churchgoers accommodate their worship to help those who come rarely get more out of it?

Chapter 8

Together in mission:
the *Five Marks of Mission*

In 1984 the Anglican Consultative Council produced a concise statement of Anglican mission applicable across the 38 diverse provinces that make up the global Anglican Communion. These *Five Marks of Mission*, adopted internationally at the 1988 Lambeth Conference, were endorsed in 1996 by the General Synod of the Church of England and have since been taken up by many dioceses as criteria against which to evaluate both existing work and new ventures. They are currently found with minor local variations of wording, but most commonly in the form developed between 1984 and 1990:

- To proclaim the good news of the kingdom
- To teach, baptise and nurture new believers
- To respond to human need by loving service
- To seek to transform unjust structures of society
- To strive to safeguard the integrity of creation and to sustain the life of the earth.[6]

The *Five Marks of Mission* featured in the preparatory Reader issued on arrival to all participating bishops in the 2008 Lambeth Conference, and underpinned one of the key themes of the gathering—'The Bishop in Mission'. The Marks are not restricted to the description of the activity of some small core religious group directed towards the world outside. Rather, they guide the Church towards identifying programmes of action to which all who would self-identify with the Christian faith can be called as both the agents of mission and the objects of mission. The wide view of mission activity that they encompass offers possibilities for engagement that might in principle attract those not easily drawn by narrower definitions; in particular they create opportunities to recruit and engage in mission tasks those who express Christian belonging but, perhaps because they belong primarily through people, places and events, are occasional rather than frequent churchgoers.

Surprisingly, despite both their widespread acceptance and recommendation for contextualisation, I found little or no evidence of anybody applying statistical methods to clarify how they might be applied. It seemed worth having a go. In particular, the responses I'd collected from my Harvest survey made it possible to look at the ways different people belong, using the model in the earlier chapters, and to reflect on what the Marks of Mission tell us might be a framework for how to engage both with and alongside the occasional churchgoers who seem to be such an important dimension of Anglican belonging. But let's first look again at the two groups of churchgoers we were introduced to in the last chapter.

Who did we find?

When the gender splits of our two groups of frequent and occasional Harvest service attendees were compared, there was no significant difference between the proportions of men and women. However, it was a different story when their ages were examined. Some 30 per cent of occasional churchgoers were aged between 20 and 49, more than twice the proportion among the regulars. The middle age range of 50 to 69 years was similar for both groups, whilst at the upper end of the scale, 20 per cent of occasional attendees were aged 70 or over compared with 35 per cent of regular churchgoers. The age distribution for the occasional churchgoers does not exhibit the strong skew towards the older end of the range that is clearly demonstrated for the weekly attendees. This might encourage us to think that an event such as Harvest Festival can have an important role to play in enabling churches to reach out towards a significantly younger group than regular activities achieve.

How do they spend their time?

We've seen that the occasional churchgoers were noticeably younger. So what do they do for a living? When asked, over a third claimed to *'hold down a demanding job'*. One in six worked from home and one in eight had a job based on *'land or agriculture'*. Patterns of church belonging and of engagement in mission that fit well with the patterns of retirement living that predominate among the regular churchgoers are not necessarily going to be readily accessible to those with demanding employment. On the other hand, working-age people may have significant mission opportunities that are not addressed by an assumption that church is part of leisure activities.

How do they fit into the local community?

A long while ago, I began to notice that there seemed a large overlap between people who were involved in church and those who I met at other events and activities in the community. The same names and faces would appear in a variety of settings. As I've set out earlier in this book, they are probably people for whom belonging through taking part in regular committed activities is more important than it is for lots of others. So how did the Harvest congregations measure in terms of getting involved in other things?

The answers I received were probably some of the most positive and encouraging in the whole of the survey. Both groups demonstrated that they were very well connected into community life.

We began with a general statement, *'There are people here I meet at other community activities'*, which sought to tease out whether the church community in general engages significantly with other local groups. Two-thirds of regular churchgoers agreed, as did well over half of the occasional ones. We noticed earlier that belonging through people scored pretty highly for the Harvest congregations. What this adds is real evidence that the relationship networks which people form are not within a closed circle, but have extensive overlaps with other contexts in which members of the local community meet. And it's not just the regular churchgoers who have these strong connections.

Community 'activity' is a pretty broad phrase. Although I've tried increasingly to restrict my own use of the word 'activity' to meetings and groups that have a regularity and sense of commitment about them, I was a bit less rigorous when I wrote the questionnaire. Almost certainly those agreeing with it would have taken a less restrictive definition, one that included summer fairs and village festivals, the things that I've tried to distinguish as 'events'.

Fortunately, the next statement, *'I am involved in other groups in this area'* puts the focus more strongly on 'activities' in my narrower sense. Unsurprisingly, for both groups the levels of agreement were lower. Among the regular churchgoers there was a small drop of seven per cent, down to three in five agreeing. For those who come to church only occasionally, the drop was much larger, down 16 per cent to just over two in five. The larger fall among the occasional churchgoers fits well with the theory we've been developing and with what we've seen earlier. It suggests that this group, who come only occasionally to church, are also less inclined to make the regular commitment to some form of group membership in the wider community. However, at two in five, it's still a large enough figure to suggest that these are not people who are completely unwilling to join in with things that may require them to commit.

There are, of course, many reasons for people not belonging to groups. Some will just lack the inclination. But it may equally be a lack of time, especially for those who said they had a demanding job. For others, particularly in less densely populated areas, it might be that they have things they would like to do as part of a group, but there aren't appropriate gatherings to join. Hence, the third statement put to the Harvest congregations, *'I enjoy community organisations'*, moved the focus from what people are actually doing now to what they believe they would enjoy doing. For the regular churchgoers there was no discernable difference from the answers to the previous question. For the occasional churchgoers it was a very different story, rising by a full 15 per cent. There are clearly a sizeable group of people coming occasionally to church who are not put off by making a commitment to an organisation, but aren't making that commitment to churchgoing. We will turn our attention more directly to what the blockages might be for some of them in the third section of this book.

The final question in this section put the spotlight firmly on the church, by inviting responses to the statement, *'Being part of the church helps me to feel at home in this community.'* I'd expected this to attract a strong level of support from the people who go to church a lot, and indeed almost three-quarters of them agreed with it. More surprising was the fact that almost half of those rarely in church also agreed. By doing so they were clearly saying two quite important things. First of all, it's a very strong statement that they do think of themselves as *'part of this church'*. That points very firmly towards their identifying primarily through the other three dimensions of our model: events, people and the place itself. Secondly, it's a declaration that belonging to the local church makes a real difference in their sense of belonging in the wider community.

Summarising occasional Harvest churchgoers

Having looked particularly at the ways in which both regular and occasional churchgoers connect to the local community, we're almost ready to set this alongside the *Five Marks of Mission* and see what avenues of approach will emerge. But let's just prepare by way of offering a short pen picture of our occasional churchgoers, both what we've explored so far in this chapter and what we've learned about them earlier on.

Our occasional attendees are much more varied in age than frequent churchgoers, and therefore more likely to be of working age. Many have demanding jobs, though only a small minority in specifically rural industries. They are well linked to the frequent churchgoers in their community through friendships, though they feel much less close to the church community as an entity. A significant minority feel well known by people in the congregation and even by the vicar. They identify strongly with the notion of having a 'family church'. Friendship plays a part for some in encouraging them to come to a church event. When they do turn up, they report the church as being welcoming. They are less likely than frequent churchgoers to have involvements in other local groups, but profess a positive attitude to community organisations, and they associate their church belonging with helping them to feel at home in the community. Place matters mostly to them because of its family associations rather than the building for its own sake. Only about half of them feel close to God in church.

With this characterisation we can now investigate how occasional churchgoers engage alongside frequent attendees, as both agents and recipients of mission activity, using the *Five Marks of Mission* as our framework.

Pastoral care

At the heart of the ecclesiology of the Church of England is the concept of the 'cure of souls' of all the people who reside in or are on the electoral roll of a parish, irrespective of their participation in church activities. It is closely related to the Mark of Mission *'Respond to human need by loving service'*. This cure resides first in the bishop but is explicitly shared with clergy at their licensings and institutions. The belief that there was once a long period of time throughout which England's parish clergy lived out this calling through personal engagement with the whole community is largely myth. It was only 19th-century reforms that began to eliminate the practice of pluralism, through which an individual could assemble a comfortable income by being incumbent of several parishes spread across the whole of England. Similar legal changes made it unlawful for the priest to live outside the benefice, unless he had the express and written agreement of the bishop. Nevertheless, the pastoral model continues to represent an important aspiration and the link to the authorisation by the bishop gives a counterbalance to congregationalism.

With the reduction in stipendiary clergy, a corresponding increase in Readers and a proliferation of formal and informal ministries, the last century, especially its final decades, has seen the priest moving to the role of convener and overseer of pastoral ministry provided by a team of lay and ordained people, rather than being the sole local supplier. Where the vicar is not resident in the immediate locality, as is the case in the majority of rural communities, that raises particular questions as to the importance of whether we can have identifiable individuals who can be seen as embodying 'the church' in each place.

What we've seen demonstrates that for many occasional churchgoers, the vicar is not only visible in the local community but also perceived as knowing his or her parishioners well. That this is still being achieved among a sizeable minority of occasional attendees, and in an era when many clergy (including most of those whose parishes were included in this survey) have been in their benefices for less than a decade, is a tribute to the pastoral dedication, hard work and skills of priests. But what we have found also makes the case for well-developed patterns of delivering pastoral care in parishes, drawing on the friendship and local community networks that embrace frequent churchgoers and their less regular counterparts, in order to build on those occasional churchgoers who already report that, *'there are people here who help me cope'* and the roughly one in three who say somebody from the church visits them at home. Much of what might be called pastoral care is delivered informally; it needs no wider authorisation and might actually suffer if it was seen to have been professionalised rather than drawing on naturally occurring links and networks. I would want to suggest, however, that from both the perspective we have been coming from and the evidence we have seen, there is considerable value in having a particular identifiable individual by whom parishioners in a specific community can feel known as part of their belonging to the church.

In terms of such formal ministries, in one or two areas the Church of England has experimented with the reintroduction of a permanent and distinctive diaconate. This has the advantage that it is an ordained ministry, and hence the person carrying it out is more easily recognised and their role understood. It may be time to assess the impact of this development to see if it could be extended more widely. Other places have, with less theological baggage, introduced the concept of 'focal ministers', who may be ordained or lay, but have a particular role of being the visible human ambassador for the church in a specific community. Whatever particular model may be followed, I would argue that the important thing is that any person chosen is one whose natural inclination is to be, and probably already is, well embedded in the networks, groups and community life of the area; somebody like my former churchwarden Mavis, to whom I introduced you much earlier.

Informal pastoral ministry already happens. What we've discovered is that with their strong sense of belonging through people, and their links within the local community, it may be some of our occasional churchgoers who are in a position to deliver it. Are they already, or can they be encouraged to become, agents of pastoral care and loving service in the community themselves? Is there scope for churches to set up schemes for pastoral care that allow participation by both regular and occasional churchgoers? Is there also a role for the church in supporting and encouraging greater levels of informal support within the community, for example by providing training? Perhaps occasional churchgoers are not just to be viewed as recipients of 'mission' but as partners in delivering it, alongside those who come to church often. Let's see if that approach can be extended to some of the other Marks.

Engaging with society and world

The Anglican *Five Marks of Mission* include the two specific commitments: 'to seek to transform unjust structures of society' and 'to strive to safeguard the integrity of creation and to sustain the life of the earth'. These are wide-reaching aspirations. They don't lie within the capacity of churches or individuals to pursue on their own, nor would it be desirable for them to try to do so. Rather, they call the church and its congregation members to work in partnership with other favorably disposed individuals and organisations.

At the local level, churches are to be found at the heart of social projects, fundraising efforts and ethical campaigns. They promote fair-trade produce, run clubs and activities for young families and older inhabitants, hold charity coffee mornings, make contributions to the secular planning process and organise door-to-door collections. The presence of occasional churchgoers at services such as Harvest, and their reported social links with others in the congregation, together provide natural opportunities for us to seek to include them in church-based or church-managed social, environmental and ethical concerns.

Individual church members themselves are often at the heart of non-church-based charities and other organisations that are working to achieve ethical and social goals; everything from the Women's Institute, local cricket club and school governors to the village hall management committee. We've seen that frequent churchgoers are very likely to be involved with these wider local community groups and to enjoy their involvement with them. Their networks of relationships are such that they meet in church with those with whom they also come into contact in other community activities.

Their preference for and enjoyment of belonging through a commitment to taking part in regular activities assists frequent churchgoers to provide the infrastructure that is needed to sustain local organisations and institutions. They are the natural officers and members of committees, the people most likely to commit to a planning group for an event, especially if it will require a regular meeting.

What their effort and commitment does is to allow others, not least our group of occasional churchgoers, who are more predisposed to one-off engagement or require a strong lead from other people, to make their own contribution as agents of this mission work. Our survey results suggest that there will be particular value in churches looking for mission actions under these two Marks of Mission that are event- or relationship-based, or linked explicitly to place. That way they will maximise the range of those who will want to take part.

What might this look like in practice?

Somebody who is drawn to belong through events and people may well be happy to host a one-off coffee morning, especially if somebody else helps with the planning and the baking. An individual with a strong connection to the place may be willing to play an important part in a campaign to improve the local environment, or help provide food for a project feeding poor children during the school summer holidays. Those who like events should be natural invitees to contribute to a Christmas fair, take part in the annual Christian Aid door-to-door collection, or come along on a protest demonstration that forms part of a wider church campaign against injustice.

Evangelism and nurture

Following the examples we've seen above, we now need to explore the extent to which occasional churchgoers, along with more regular ones, can be both recipients of and partners in the work of the church in evangelism and nurture. Within the *Five Marks of Mission* these two elements are expressed as, 'to proclaim the good news of the kingdom' and, 'to teach, baptise and nurture new believers'.

The strength of friendship links found in the Harvest survey establishes the value of personal relationships as a key component of proclaiming the gospel and nurturing believers. Many churches work with the grain of this, basing their mission strategies on the tenet that friendship is the most common route to joining a church. Where courses such as Alpha and Emmaus are used, it may be advisable to encourage attendance through friendship or family links rather than through general advertisement. Indeed, when I used Alpha courses for several years as a vicar, the most notable success was in bringing into regular church membership and deeper faith a group of younger dads whose wives and partners were already committed and involved. Fortunately there were enough of them to form their own peer group where friendships were built and sustained.

In addition, the value put on place, and in particular the association of place with family, suggests that careful thought as to how buildings are presented and interpreted will also have a significant role to play in both gospel proclamation and nurturing of occasional churchgoers. Congregations that are forever giving out the message that their building is a millstone around their necks are unlikely to be heard positively by those who have strong connections to it. However, I have known apparently non-evangelistic engagements, such as involving occasional churchgoers in buildings projects, become an effective tool for outreach.

It is important, whilst we are discussing evangelism and nurture, that we remember that the model underlying this book cautions against a simple equation of successful proclamation and nurture with increased attendance at weekly services or membership of church groups. For some that will undoubtedly be the case—a predisposition to event-based belonging does not preclude becoming committed to activities—but for many, the outcome of successful work on these two Marks of Mission will be a group of occasional churchgoers who have a better understanding of and commitment to their faith, which they act out through diverse and often one-off engagements in and beyond the local community, who access the church for pastoral support, feel connected to its public leadership and are willing to support it financially on a more frequent and more generous, if episodic, basis.

It is also important to note that the occasional churchgoers, whose faith is supported by relationships, places and events rather than activities, have something here to teach frequent attendees about the importance of diversity in how Christian faith is lived out and expressed. Part of the process of growing in Christian maturity is an increasing recognition of the faith of others; the proclamation of this gospel truth by our occasional group to their frequent churchgoing counterparts is mission in its full sense.

What can we conclude?

The evidence we've found of a rich and complex pattern of belonging challenges the often implicit assumption that occasional churchgoers are 'nominal' Christians, a premise which underpins much current writing and thinking on mission. In its place we have established the notion that these are Christians who express their belonging to God and Christ in different and less easily numerically assessed ways from the present dominant model of regular Sunday worship and involvement in church groups and committees.

Taking part alongside regular churchgoers in the performance of the *Five Marks of Mission* in the ways we've described represents a significant level of commitment, a real belonging to the local church and a genuine participation in the task of Christian discipleship on the part of occasional churchgoers. Putting the opportunities for such at the heart of the life of the local church is not a means of inoculating individuals against a proper personal commitment to Christ, but rather recognises that for some people such commitment is expressed differently. If occasional churchgoers understand, express and live out their faith in a less articulate fashion than frequent churchgoers, this may be more to do with the systemic failure of churches to engage seriously with them on their own territory, rather than indicative of a lesser commitment to what they consider it is to be Christian.

Those who come to the rural Harvest service and other occasional church events, including through a regular pattern of attendance at baptisms, marriages and funerals in the parish, are amenable to living out the *Five Marks of Mission* of the Anglican Communion. Drawing them in to such a programme of involvement may help demonstrate a model of church that is not simply one where the professional religious are the agents and the laity are reduced to being recipients or consumers of religion. Indeed, it may be the fact that churchgoing is seen as a largely passive activity that deters some from attending more frequently.

Finally, I'm increasingly convinced that when the local church pays proper attention to the ways in which people belong, that will help some individuals to move through areas of engagement to which they find it easier to commit towards a wider involvement in the life of the local church, including more frequent participation in its regular worship.

Questions

- Do the *Five Marks of Mission* set a good agenda for the local church to follow? Is there anything missing from them?

- Can I think of examples of where people have come to a deeper faith through engaging in a practical piece of action in the community?

- When we are organising things in our church, could we look wider at who might be involved in them?

- Has my own faith grown through engaging in mission? If so, what made the difference?

Chapter 9

Paying the piper:
what has become of Anglican
governance and finance?

I ended the first section of this book with something I called a 'worked example'. We looked at how the fourfold model of belonging might be used to explore a particular issue; in that case, the questions provoked by the increasing use of Communion by Extension as a response to a lack of availability of priests that had developed over time. I want to do something similar to end this second section, but to turn attention to a very different subject. We've been focused on the question of mission; but who takes the decisions that drive local church mission, and how is it funded?

Governing the church

At several points I've drawn attention in what I've been writing to the fact that Parochial Church Councils and others with responsibility for planning and delivering Anglican worship and church programmes are most likely to be those who enjoy regular meetings and hence belong principally, or at least substantially, through activities. The risk of any such group taking decisions that affect others is that they may either fail to understand that other people belong in ways different from themselves, or not recognise these different dimensions of belonging as being genuine expressions of Christian faith and identity.

What I'd like to suggest is that the model we've been considering, of belonging through activities, people, places and events, gives us a means of exploring more deeply this phenomenon of governance by committee, especially in the light of where the Church of England has come from over the last century and more.

Prior to the formation of Parochial Church Councils in the early 20th century, the annual Vestry Meeting lay at the centre of church governance. Here the people would elect one or two churchwardens. Until the Victorian era, it was also when the annual parish church rate, a legally enforceable tax, would be determined. The meeting was open to all qualified to vote in secular elections. It was clearly an 'event' in the framework of the fourfold model. Indeed, it was the attendance and participation of non-churchgoers at the Vestry Meeting which led to the setting of zero rates and the collapse and eventual abolition of the rate system of church funding. By contrast, the modern-day Annual Meeting of a Church of England parish has a limited range of functions and powers which are broadly similar to those of the AGM of a company or charity and, except for the appointment of churchwardens, the qualification to vote is restricted to those on the Church Electoral Roll.

Throughout my own time as a parish priest, we maintained the pattern of the Annual Meeting as a free-standing event. In one typical church, it took place on a weekday evening, separate from any of the normal times of public worship. It was normally preceded by a brief act of worship and then followed by a substantial bring and share supper, sometimes with entertainment provided. All the reports were written, collated into a booklet, and made available in church at least the previous weekend. If I was doing it now, I would probably publish them on a parish webpage as well. Members of the midweek congregation as well as those from the various Sunday services were equally welcome. The supper gave a good excuse for regular churchgoers to bring along family members.

The context of the meeting made it more than possible for some robust challenges to be made and responded to. I knew that I had to give account of myself through my vicar's report and be ready to face difficult questions. Sometimes the cut and thrust of the conversation was what helped me to give a better account of how I was spending my

time and energies. Sometimes it was what helped me to reassess and
do things differently.

What I've noticed, however, especially in more recent years, is that
parishes have increasingly moved to holding the meeting either directly
after or even during the principle service on a Sunday morning. I can
understand the logic. This is the time when most of those who would
want to come to an Annual Meeting are in church anyway, but it turns
it from an event to something ancillary to an activity. I'm not sure that
those who felt able to put hard questions to me on a Tuesday evening
would have felt quite so willing to come and do so after I had just
presided at the Eucharist, and certainly not during the middle of it. I've
also known of cases where a church Annual Meeting has been a packed
and difficult event, with conflicting factions ranged against each
other, and appropriately so. I suspect that on a Sunday morning the
necessary critical voices would have been at least considerably muted
and more likely absent. The message, although I'm sure it is hardly
ever intended as such, would appear to be that the Annual Meeting is
not there to exercise any form of accountability from those who hold
office, lay or ordained, but is simply an occasion for those who belong
through activity to elect individuals similar to themselves to oversee
the church. Governance through event has significantly diminished.

Look around any of our older church buildings and you are likely to
find somewhere in it a plaque commemorating some major extension,
addition or restoration. In most cases it will contain three names,
the incumbent of the day and the two churchwardens. The office of
churchwarden is an ancient one. It has clearly changed significantly
over the centuries; nevertheless, the principle that the wardens are
appointed jointly by the incumbent and the parishioners to work
primarily with the former, but not simply to be the vicar's servants, still
stands. Wardens are admitted to office usually by the archdeacon on
behalf of the bishop. They are officers of both bishop and crown, as the
twin tops to their staves testify. They promise to bring to the attention
of the bishop any matters or persons of which he or she needs to
know. Whether or not it is still the case, I was once told that within

the curtilage of the church the warden has the powers of a constable. Until quite recently it was the wardens who exercised the rights of the parish in accepting or rejecting the nomination by the patron of a new incumbent; a role that has now passed to representatives elected by the church council.

With the creation and rise of the church council, the role of the churchwardens has undergone considerable change. That doesn't mean it has got easier; indeed, with the huge demands and expectation laid on many wardens nowadays, it has ceased to surprise me when smaller parishes are unable to find two people both prepared to stand. But the governance side has probably diminished even as the practical side has expanded. Historically, the wardens were primarily people of note and standing within the parish. They would have been individuals clearly identified with the church to such an extent that their network of relationships would have been likely to contain and sustain a strong element of belonging through them as people. Nowadays, where a warden does carry such a load of belonging with them, it can make it even harder for the role to be passed on to anybody else.

The extent to which some wardens continue to provide a channel of belonging, and to provide it for those who are not primarily attracted to belong to the church through activities, is a topic that I'm sure would repay further study. By and large, however, it is likely that with the change in the governance role of the churchwarden, the influence through people of those who prefer to belong in that way is less now than in earlier times.

The picture with regard to belonging through place presents a more complex situation. Whilst the Vestry Meeting has long since ceased to serve as a gathering of all the inhabitants of the parish, recent years have seen the development of friends' groups in a number of places. Legally separate from the church council, these have provided a way to strengthen the structures through which those who wish to support the fabric of a particular church can do so without being drawn into the governance or participation in other aspects of the church programme.

They can meet 'as required' rather than having a regular and frequent cycle. It is plausible that as such, they may be more likely to be led by those who appreciate the value of one-off events and their distinctive appeal, than is the case for the church council. Such groups, though, are not always entirely benign. Where the money raised by them has become an essential element in the budget for maintaining the church building, and where powerful personalities have been in charge of them, it has not been unknown for the 'friends' to seek to exercise a veto over matters, such as styles of worship in the church, that lie well outside of their remit.

Whilst parishes seem to have moved steadily in one direction, there is good evidence, outside of church circles, to suggest that in other parts of the British establishment, governance by a committee of activists has passed its heyday and is being replaced by a model that makes more of an effort to engage with all four dimensions of belonging.

Successive national UK governments have sought in recent years to reintroduce the personal element to local services in England. Some of these initiatives have been more successful than others. A first move was towards 'cabinet and scrutiny' structures in local authorities, giving more direct accountability and power to named individuals instead of committees. These are now pretty universal. The second trend has been the promotion of directly elected mayors. With the exception of London, these have proved much less popular; many communities invited to vote on whether to have a mayor have given it a firm thumbs down. In some cases, the system threw up unlikely winners, though it is widely held that a man who was elected first time round as a joke candidate dressed in a monkey costume became quite a capable politician and leader in due course. It remains to be seen whether attaching a requirement for an elected mayor to any devolution agreement for English city regions, beginning with Greater Manchester, will revive the concept. The third area in which government has attempted to move to putting a named person to the fore is with the appointment of police and crime commissioners in the early 2010s. These got off to a very poor start by electoral standards, with a derisory turnout in many parts of the country. However, the visibility of the commissioners, replacing the largely anonymous police authorities that went before them, has shown some evidence of creating a level of accountability that had previously been absent.

The extension of event-based governance has chiefly been through local authorities and others wishing to make major changes (for example, to the management structures for council housing) being required to demonstrate a thorough process of consultation which reaches, via one-off occasions, beyond the activists. The nearest equivalent in church circles, the requirement that certain major national decisions require a majority of diocesan synods to vote in favour of them, doesn't really take us beyond the circles of the most active, not even if the diocese in turn invites each deanery synod to debate the topic.

The Localism Act 2011 had at its heart the intention to put decisions affecting particular places more into the hands of those who live in or care about them. The extent to which these political aims are being achieved may be open to question, but the intention to extend governance in directions that can be seen to include all four dimensions is not.

Comparing the direction of travel of Church and state has, I hope, shown that the trends do not always have to be in the direction of 'government by the activist for the activist'. I'm not a constitutional expert and would have no idea how church governance might be reconstructed on a national scale to restore the lost balance. But what I hope to have achieved is maybe to start a conversation at some local levels. What are the informal ways that each of our own churches might consider that would allow the voices of those who belong with us through people, place and event to be heard, and given due weight?

Raising and spending the money

Since I started reflecting on the nature of Christian belonging, and especially when I began to share some of my findings with church groups, one particular issue kept coming back to me. Whilst it may be desirable to operate with a wider view of belonging than simply regular church attendance, it is the latter which enables the bills to be paid. Successful pastoral and mission work that results in people who don't come very often to church strengthening their links through people, events and the place, but still only turning up occasionally to a regular service, is likely to cost more than it raises. And the people paying that cost will be those who have made the regular commitment.

Once again, it's worth starting with the history. How did we get to the present model of funding churches and their ministry?

Just as with church governance, there has been a huge move in the way in which the mission and ministry of the Church of England is financed through the course of the last century; and again it is a move in the direction of activity belonging. Clergy stipends, though supplemented by fees for funerals, weddings etc. and the Easter Offering, were historically much more based on the place, being paid through the income of the benefice itself. This included the glebe rents received from lands that had been vested in the Church at the time of the Enclosure Acts, in lieu of tithes. Incumbents in less well-endowed parishes had their income supplemented through funds such as Queen Anne's Bounty, now part of the Church Commissioners. Priests who retired were entitled to a proportion of the benefice income for the rest of their lives. Curates were largely paid from the incumbent's own resources or via charities such as the Additional Curates Society, some of which are still operating. Upkeep of the church building was split between the rector, who had responsibility for the chancel, and the parishioners, whose church rates, levied by decision of the annual Vestry Meeting, were, as well as paying for other local necessities, to keep the nave in good condition.

Glebe income, which bore no relation to the size of the parish or the demands placed on the incumbent, was transferred to dioceses in the 1970s, in order to allow for the standardisation of stipend levels. Church rates, as we've already mentioned, disappeared somewhat earlier, as the rise in the number of non-conformists led to an increasing reluctance to pay for what they were not receiving benefit from. The agreements that have allowed church taxes to continue to this day in large parts of northern Europe were never applied to England. Place-based income generation is now largely through the friends' groups mentioned in the previous section.

The connection between clergy income and belonging through events has also been severed. At one time the Easter Offering was for the personal income of the incumbent priest. Whilst it may remain the case that some parishes seek to continue the tradition informally, the rules are quite clear that any such income should be netted off the stipend. Curates' stipends have long ceased to be paid from the incumbent's pocket. In 1913 my predecessor as Bishop of Manchester made his first appeal for payment of what we would now call Parish Share.

Chancel repair liability remains the last area where financial responsibility for the upkeep of the church or its ministry lies with a specified individual. Often attached to the ownership of a specific piece of land within the parish, its levying has proved increasingly contentious in recent times. The potential damage to relationships in the local community, if the residents on a certain housing development or the owner of a particular farm are presented with a bill for a new roof, means that in many parishes decisions have been taken not to register the liability before a cut-off date set by the government. As with church rates, it is hard in the present culture to argue that payment should be disconnected from the receiving of benefit.

In place of these historic sources of income that respectively linked to event, place and relationship, churches have developed financial models based strongly on 'planned giving' schemes in which regular churchgoers commit themselves to a set amount each week or month and are invited to revise (and increase) their giving on an annual basis. Many churches would now take it as a matter of principle that this is the proper route to fund mission and ministry. If ministry is to be supported and sustained across the poorest as well as wealthiest parts of the diocese, this almost inevitably requires some parishes to contribute a level of Share that exceeds what they receive in return. Unsurprisingly, that is not always popular. Giving a regular amount weekly or monthly fits well with a pattern of attending church functions on a similarly regular basis. It hasn't proved obvious how this might be effectively extended to those who belong in other ways.

Event-based income generation still remains significant. Most major repairs and improvements to churches are funded outside the regular income, through appeals and events in the community. People who have a sense of identification with the building remain generous in contributing to the costs of specific identified works. Those who enjoy church events will throw themselves into special occasions in aid of the appeal.

Event-based income also continues to make a significant contribution to the regular income of many churches. Many villages in particular have held on to the practice of generating a substantial portion of income from special events such as fairs and fetes. Such occasions can be the highlights of the local community year, an expression of shared belonging that has the church at its centre but which is not only attended by the wider community but staffed by it too. In some places (for example the well dressings of Derbyshire or the scarecrow festivals and open village weekends of Worcestershire), there has been a revival of village-wide events that are held to raise church funds. The income from these is not normally restricted to the maintenance of buildings, but forms part of the monies that can be applied for general purposes.

The thrust of what we've found would suggest that belonging through participation in church social events is not to be underestimated, and that it should properly be seen as part of the funding as well as the mission strategy; but the use of event funding for regular church income carries with it two significant areas of risk.

Almost every vicar will have spent sleepless nights, praying that the forecast downpour will not result in the abandonment of the Annual Summer Fair, and a consequent loss of income. On one occasion, a small parish in my benefice was bailed out on the day itself by the friendly landlady of the village pub (a tribute to the importance of strong relationships) turning over the premises to us for the Saturday afternoon. The risks of weather are obvious, though a decent plan of spreading them across several events through the course of the year can go some way to mitigating the loss of any particular occasion.

Less obvious are the risks that come from a declining relationship with the wider community whose support is necessary for the event to succeed. But I want to take quite a radical line on this. A core component of Christian theology is the concept of appropriate vulnerability. As the followers of the one who made himself weak for our sakes, we are not called to find ourselves a place secure from all risk, but to follow in his example. A local church that has no need or requirement for the goodwill of the community in which it is situated has, to my thinking, lost the plot. Invulnerability, by its very nature, tends to build barriers around itself.

Of course, churches should be prepared to take difficult decisions over anything from graveyard regulations to supporting a planning application for social housing. At the same time, clergy must be strong and confident enough to preach and teach aspects of the faith that may not accord with general public opinion in the parish. But it's right and proper that there should be a cost to taking such stances, and that the cost should fall primarily on those who have made the decision or are most closely aligned with the opinion being promulgated. They are the ones who need to be prepared to make up any consequent shortfall in income from their own pockets. At the very least this would act as a spur to explaining to the wider community why they have taken the position that they have.

In addition to the work of friends' groups, as mentioned above, there are just the beginnings of a move towards a revival of more place-based income generation in churches. At the heart of this lies the belief that the church building is not exclusively for staging acts of worship, but is to work and witness through being the venue for a much wider range of occasions. It represents something of a return to the medieval practice of the nave being the place where almost all community events took place. Post-Reformation, with the advent of fixed pews as the proper setting for attending to lengthy sermons, and a stronger distinction between sacred and secular, the Church largely ceased to function in its former way. Now, the increasing use of moveable seating is allowing a recovery of what has been lost. If the church can be arranged 'café-style' for a special service on Sunday, is there any reason why it can't be arranged in the same style for the cricket club awards dinner on Friday night?

The key theological principle at stake here is about what happens when the sacred and the secular are mixed. Are we operating with a theology of contamination or sanctification? If it's the former, then holding events in the church that are not explicitly religious in flavour risks desecrating the worship space. If it's the latter, then this may be an opportunity to allow the building to speak of the glory of God to those who have come with more earthly matters at the forefront of their minds. Whilst I like to be even-handed, it's probably clear that I would put myself in the second category.

It's a line we have consistently been taking in Manchester Cathedral in recent years. The very shape of the building draws the eyes naturally upwards towards an architecture that speaks of the divine. When this is enhanced by skilful lighting and the addition of appropriate furnishings and decorations, the effect is stunning. Manchester people are able to offer up their best, in arts and music, in a setting that provides a constant, if for many of those present, subliminal, reminder that the gifts we have and offer come from the one who makes and redeems us. It struck me most strongly when handing out an award at the city's annual business dinner. We were celebrating the excellence of human achievement in a place that reminded us that there is something greater even than humanity. I've spoken to people whose first experience of the inside of the building has been for such a community occasion, but who, having found themselves welcomed and at home within it, have returned. Such events raise money that can then support both regular ministry and the improvement of the building for those who are beginning to belong through it. But I would also class them as genuine missional outreach.

If it is possible to raise funds through places and events, what about the final dimension of our model: people? On a small scale, it's something that has been going on for a long while. I can no longer remember when and what was the first sponsored event I undertook as a clergyman, but it must have been many years ago. In 2013, I was part of a small group that climbed Kilimanjaro in aid of maternity provision at a rural hospital in Tanzania. The next year I joined a collection of clergy who went on the scariest ride in Blackpool Pleasure Beach to support the work of the Children's Society. In each case, my sponsors were supporting both the cause and me. I would argue that the act of donating money to somebody undertaking a personal challenge, even if a slightly silly one, is both based on and then builds the sense of belonging that that donor has with the person to whose effort they are contributing. People who have supported my sponsored task feel closer to me. It is likely that the sums raised through personal sponsorship are almost always going to be relatively small, and mostly directed not at core church funding but towards special appeals. As such they may not merit a large entry on the church's budget sheet. But they serve as evidence again that raising money from those who belong through people, places and events both is possible and can enhance belonging.

Questions

- Should the costs of the local church fall entirely on its congregation? If not, in what ways is it justified to ask others to contribute?

- Should church councils give greater weight to the views of occasional churchgoers? How might they do so?

- Is the Church of England steadily turning into a sect? If so, is that a good or a bad thing?

- Should an incumbent still have the right to choose one of the churchwardens?

Part Three   **Who else is missing?**

Introduction

Most of this book has been exploring one particular aspect of the theology of individual differences; we've tried to engage with people whose primary belonging is through people, places, activities and events. But, as mentioned in the Introduction, this is an area of theology that goes much wider. In the next couple of chapters I want to share two other aspects of individual difference that I was able to explore through the cathedral carol service survey in Worcester.

Many, especially clergy, will have come across the concept of Psychological Type, especially as explored through what is often referred to as the Myers-Briggs test. It has been used very widely to help people understand why they prefer to operate in particular ways, and even to suggest the types of prayer that are most likely to appeal to each of the sixteen distinct types.

Religious Orientation will be a less familiar concept to most. It began in the 1940s as a way of grappling with questions around the persistence of prejudice among followers of religions that appeared to preach tolerance. By contrast with Psychological Type, it offers us a position on each of three continuous scales that measure different dimensions of what motivates us in our religious beliefs and practices. Over the intervening years, as the model has grown, and as ways of determining it through questionnaires have been tested and proven, it has been found to be a powerful predictor of how religious people are likely to respond to certain types of issues.

It's clearly useful for me as an individual to know my own personal type and to have an understanding of the balance of motivations behind my engagement with my faith. But populations, including church congregations, are made up of aggregations of individuals. Does a church have a distinctive type or orientation? Are the people found in its services a broad representation of the population of its parish, or is some unseen sifting taking place?

I'd like to whet your appetites for both of these ways of distinguishing between people and their religiosity. But then our focus will be on whether there are particular groups that regular church services are not reaching. If so, then that raises the question as to whether both the event and activity aspects of the things we do as a church can be adjusted in ways that will broaden their appeal. Can we include more of those who are made in God's image, even if that image differs invisibly from its representation in you or me?

Chapter 10

Types and temperaments: what is Psychological Type?

It was some time in the early 1990s; I was travelling with my wife on a train to Manchester. We had time to spare and fell to discussing what we might do about a summer holiday. Several times we nearly made a decision, but on each occasion I came up with a new idea, or some extra information that we hadn't fully considered. I was enjoying the conversation; she was clearly getting more and more frustrated by it. The reason for our journey was that we had both undertaken a Myers-Briggs test. One of the cathedral canons was putting on a day in which a large group of us would be given our individual results, our Psychological Type, and then be told what it meant about our preferred ways of engaging. About halfway through the day, as an illustration of the difference between one particular pair of Type Indicators, he used the example of a couple struggling to decide where to go on holiday; not as a consequence of them preferring very different destinations, but because whilst one would always be trying to make a choice, the other would forever be bringing in new things to consider. He could have been listening to us in our carriage. Not surprisingly, after that I got interested in the theory behind it.

We're all used to being measured on scales, sometimes literally. One person is heavier than another, or taller, or has better hearing. What is relatively unusual about Psychological Type theory is that the categories to which we belong are composed of polar opposites. It's not interested in whether somebody is very extravert, or just a little bit. It's sufficient for the theory to distinguish between those who are basically extravert and those who are introvert. In fact that particular pairing of extraversion, symbolised by the letter [E], and introversion, symbolised by [I], called the 'orientation', is the first of four similar pairings which together make up the four-letter sequence that is an individual's Type. The next pairing is called the 'perceiving process'. When we are engaging with the world around us, do we prefer sensing [S] or intuition [N]? The two 'judging processes', thinking [T] and feeling [F], describe whether it's our thoughts or our emotions that play the greater part in helping us reach a decision. Lastly, and back to my train journey, are the two attitudes, judging [J] and perceiving [P]. These tell us, when we are engaging with the outside world, which of the two processes we've just described we are going to prefer to go with.

The set of four attributes, written as a series of four capital letters, for any individual is referred to as the person's 'Type'. The theory has been around for a long time; it has its origins in the work of Carl Jung. The standard model, now well tested and referred to as the Myers-Briggs Type Indicator® (MBTI®), has been around since at least the mid-1980s.

One of the first things that was discovered about Type is that the standard results are very different between men and women. That means it's necessary to investigate each sex separately, although the same set of questions are used for both sexes. Similarly, as studies of Psychological Type show different proportions of the various types in different countries, it is necessary to compare with other samples from the same nation, and in particular with the norms for the general population. Type theory has been used across a wide range of contexts, for example to help members of a workplace team understand how they fit together, and to make them aware of how their own preferred patterns of behaviour might frustrate colleagues in the same way that my way of discussing holidays frustrated my wife. Other sorts of psychological instruments have been developed; the commercial world in particular plays host to many, but Type seems to have been particularly adopted in church circles. Part of the attraction may be that, unlike with some business scales, there isn't a preferred sort of person to be. Intuition isn't better than Sensing, Feeling isn't in some way more Christian than Thinking. With the eight letters listed, it's possible for you or me to be any one of 16 distinct types, and all of them are of equal merit.

The full MBTI® test is well worth undertaking if you want to know your individual Type. Indeed, it might be, after reading this, that you want to go and do just that. Unfortunately, there are a couple of drawbacks when it comes to using it for a statistical study. It's quite long, and it may well be that many of the participants wouldn't want to spend that amount of time completing it, especially when it's only one part of a much bigger questionnaire. It's also quite expensive to administer. The good news is that such a long set of questions isn't really necessary when what we're wanting to do is not to identify accurately the qualities of specific people, but to compare populations. To cope with this issue, alternative forms of ascribing a specific Type to an individual have been developed. For the purposes of the present research, the Francis Psychological Type Scales (FPTS)[7] were used. These have been developed, tested and found to work well in relationship to the field of Empirical Theology. What's more, they've been used in a number of recent studies of regular churchgoers in the UK, which helps us when it comes to making comparisons with the people who filled in the cathedral survey.

Type and churchgoers

Before we get on to the cathedral people, what are the key facts about churchgoers, clergy and lay congregation members, which have emerged from research?

Two fairly large studies of those in ordained ministry have built up a picture which shows that among male Church of England clergy there are considerably higher proportions of i[N]tuitives than in the general male population. In fact, at 64 per cent there are more than twice as many. The same is true, though not quite to such a large extent, when it comes to counting the [F]eeling and [J]udging types, where the differences are 20 and 15 percentage points, respectively.

Research into female clergy is less developed as yet, because women have only been ordained in UK Anglican churches for a relatively short period of time, and in consequence there have been fewer of them available to study. Tentative results, however, would suggest that female clergy are more [I]ntrovert and hugely more i[N]tuitive than women in the population. There are no significant differences on the other two scales.

Among laymen in church, research has found higher proportions of [I]ntroverts, [S]ensing, [F]eeling and [J]udging types than in the country at large. The [J] difference is by far the largest, up by over 30 percentage points to 86 per cent, whilst the others' differences lie between seven and nine percentage points.

Among laywomen there are significantly higher proportions of [I]ntroverts and [J]udging types than in the general population. Again, it's the [J] figure where the difference is the greatest, as with the men in church; this takes the total of [J] types in the sample to five out of every six. The [I] figure is a little higher than the population norm too. By contrast with their male counterparts, there are no significant differences in terms of churchgoing women's preferences for [S]ensing/ i[N]tuiting or [F]eeling/[T]hinking.

The differences between the Type profile of churchgoers and that of adults in general poses important questions. If we believe that the missional call of the Church is not just to fill it with more people like ourselves, then we need to know who it is that we are, disproportionately, failing to reach. It may be that in some cases there's nothing we can do about it, but that should be a decision we take having been informed of the facts, not something we fall into through ignorance. So what interested me was whether the cathedral carol service, a very different style of service from what goes on in most churches most of the time, and which clearly attracts quite a large proportion of people who are not seen often at other services, was simply reflecting the same types as turn up on a Sunday. Alternatively, might it be appealing to a group that looks more like a cross section of the population at large?

I suppose I ought to admit that perhaps part of my interest in underrepresented types at church services may be because my own type is ENTP which, you will probably gather from the figures I've quoted, makes me fairly unusual among churchgoers. But let's now look at some of the differences in more detail, and see what the cathedral congregation had to tell us.

Thinking and feeling

Within the general population, the greatest Type difference between the sexes is that whilst only 35 per cent of men prefer [F]eeling to [T]hinking, the figure doubles to 70 per cent for women. But what's the difference between the two types? In a paper by Francis, Robbins and Craig, it was put like this:

> For thinking types the preferred way of judging is through objective analysis and dispassionate logic. They are concerned with the good running of systems and organisations and put such strategic issues first. They are logical and fair-minded people who are attracted to the God of justice.[8]

By contrast:

> For feeling types the preferred way of judging is through subjective evaluation and personal involvement. They are concerned with good relationships between people and put such interpersonal issues first. They are humane and warm-hearted people who are attracted to the God of mercy.[9]

Whichever Type you are, I would expect you might recognise something of yourself in those descriptions.

One of the things we know about church congregations is that there are on average about two women present for every man. I've already said that the [F] figure for male clergy is high; at 55 per cent it's closer to the 70 per cent norm for women than the 35 per cent average for men. The [F] figure for women in church congregations is exactly in line with the wider population. In other words, men in church are surrounded by predominantly [F] types, both in the congregation around them and by those who are leading the worship and the wider activities of the church. In that context, it's not a great surprise that the figures for feeling types among men in church congregations were 42 per cent, not the 35 per cent in the general population. When it came to the cathedral, a rather different picture emerged. Among men, the [F] types were down to 31 per cent and among women they were down to 61 per cent, both not only below the Sunday congregation figures, but less than found in the general population. There's something about the carol service that is appealing to the [T] type rather more than regular services achieve.

At first glance, it is not at all obvious why a cathedral carol service should appeal to those who prefer 'objective analysis and dispassionate logic' to 'good relationships and interpersonal issues'. It may be important to set the cathedral carol service within the wider context of Christmas worship. Apart from the carol service, the other special services offered around Christmas in Anglican parishes comprise predominantly of Christingle services, nativity services, family services and Midnight Mass. When compared with the structure of the carol service, each of these might be seen to have a more strongly relational atmosphere. Hence, it is plausible that the carol service provides a distinctive opportunity which, whilst it makes no direct appeal to logic or analysis, is not couched in a context of emotional and relational engagement and that a service that is not cast in a 'feeling' idiom will attract the thinking Type even without the need to cater explicitly for their preferred judging process. It may even be the case that because the wider celebration of Christmas, in the family home, at parties and social events, is more strongly allied with a preference for the relational rather than the logical, the cathedral, and some church carol services, offer a much-needed haven for the [T] person in the middle of an otherwise overwhelmingly [F] season.

I mentioned a little earlier that over half of male Anglican clergy were seen to have a preference for feeling. Alongside this, the increasing numbers of women clergy are drawn from a population with around 70 per cent sharing the same preference. We know that congregations are made up of men and women who also show a greater preference for feeling than the cathedral sample (42 per cent and 70 per cent respectively). Taken together, what this suggests to me is that by and large, Church of England services are planned and led by [F]eeling types who, unless they make a particular effort to the contrary, will have a predisposition to assume that the idiom that works for them is the one to use when devising special occasions. I'd want to argue that the traditional Nine Lessons and Carols shape of the cathedral service predates a steady move towards a more [F] style of worship in the Church of England. Family services, with which category Christingle and nativity services have a great deal in common, are naturally skewed in a relational direction. Add to this the almost complete replacement of Morning Prayer by Holy Communion, and the ways in which the eucharistic liturgy has been revised since the 1960s, not least the incorporation into it of the Sharing of the Peace, and it all seems like a move in the same [F] direction. None of that is to line myself up against a series of changes that have been, in my view, healthy and appropriate. Rather, it is to say that allowing our liturgy to develop in the way that it has over several decades leaves us with an awkward question to face about what kind of provision we could or should make in our worship for those who are of a [T]hinking type.

I believe that there are several ways in which we can go about this. One is simply to fit into the Church calendar, through the course of the year, a small number of one-off events that are deliberately cast in a mould designed to appeal to a [T] person. A more substantial response is to look at the elements in our main regular acts of worship that are not part of the set liturgy and can be structured to be a bit more Type inclusive. I'm thinking especially about sermons and hymns.

Church music remains one of the most challenging things to get right. In my experience, it provokes more arguments and anger than anything except throwing out the pews. In one parish where I was vicar, both those who strongly preferred traditional hymns and the fans of modern worship songs were happy to compromise, as long as their favoured style formed a clear majority of what we were singing at each service. Just as there are good and bad songs among both the old and the new, there are hymns and songs that are couched in language that is more relational or more logical. I'm sure that as a [T] Type, my natural inclination was towards the latter, which may have meant that in churches where I chose the music, more of the hymns were of that category. My guess is that if predominantly [F] leaders simply pick the music that works best for them and for their predominantly [F] congregations, they are missing an important trick.

In the same way, I think there is a challenge to those charged with preaching. We ought to produce sermons at least some of the time that are deliberately planned to appeal to types other than their own. When I was first involved in leading Alpha courses, I soon found that there was one set of people who really warmed to the long talk, sprinkled heavily with facts and figures, and another which responded well to the later groups, where feelings and experiences were shared. Most of the men came in the first category. It was the communal meal, sandwiched between the talk and the groups that held everyone together. I remember taking a deliberate decision that, once every so often, it would be important for me to preach a sermon that was styled like the talks that were bringing these people into faith and Church.

The 'Guardian' temperament

The research I've referred to earlier in this chapter has shown that regular Church of England churchgoers are heavily weighted towards being both [S]ensing and [J]udging types. It's not surprising, then, that many are both. Indeed, among English Anglican congregations, the [SJ] people were found to be 71 per cent of the men and 73 per cent of the women. This is a long way above the percentages found in the general UK population, which are 44 per cent for men and 54 per cent for women. At the cathedral carol service, the results were a little lower than the wider church figures, at 62 per cent of men and 68 per cent of women. But this is still very significantly above what we would expect from a random selection of individuals.

The [SJ] combination is often referred to by the descriptor 'Guardian'. It's a slightly confusing term in British circles, where to describe someone as a *'Guardian* type' would normally be taken to refer to a reader of the main quality left of centre daily newspaper. Within the language of Psychological Type Theory, it takes a very different definition.

The 'Guardian Temperament' is characterised as one that honours customs and traditions and seeks familiarity and stability in a fast-changing world. Those of this temperament tend to join groups and to be hard-working, loyal and dutiful, not least in sustaining social institutions such as churches. With such a characterisation, it is not surprising that they are found in relatively large numbers in church congregations. From what we have found in this book, we would expect people like this to be more inclined to make the commitment to what we have called 'activities' than we would others. Those who are not Guardians by nature may be more likely to express religious belonging through people, places or events.

This then adds to what we have already found about how churches are substantially populated and led by people who are not fully representative of the wider community. Guardians are more likely to serve on church committees and councils and hence to take a strong part in planning and delivering mission and ministry. But alongside and often leading the laypeople who make up church committees are the clergy. And here the picture is a very different one. Among both male and female clergy there is a very much lower proportion of [S]ensing types, less than half as many. At the same time, clergy of both sexes are more than twice as likely to be [P]erceiving (the alternative to [J]) than their congregation members. I haven't been able to find direct figures for the [SJ] combination among clergy, but on the basis of the numbers for the separate components and by comparing with the distributions for the general population, churchgoers and cathedral carol service congregations, it would seem likely to be just below 30 per cent for both men and women.

What this paints for us is a picture of a church where the clergy are likely to be far more positively inclined towards change and innovation than the laypeople who attend their services and work with them in overseeing mission and ministry. I've always been someone who delights in finding God in unexpected places, who enjoys being encouraged to think differently about something, and who thinks that the most settled situations would be improved if a little bit of chaos were thrown in. Working with church councils and synods with a predominant Guardian temperament has brought its challenges. The popular joke, that the Church of England is like a car with the engine of a lawnmower and the brakes of a juggernaut, probably owes much to the fact that its legislation, policy and practice is produced through bodies and committees with strong Guardian representation.

This is not an argument to call on Guardians to stand down from their positions of responsibility. They are exactly the sort of people who run things diligently and well. As elsewhere in this book, it's a call for all of us who hold responsibility for taking decisions that affect the wider Church to be aware that our own particular standpoint and preferences are much less the norm among our wider church and local community than we might want to imagine; and then to temper our decisions in the light of this self-understanding. Maybe it suggests that we ought to give the vicar a little more leeway in coming up with and implementing new ideas for mission and ministry, or new styles of service that complement and extend the range of what already exists. And in particular, the huge difference between the figures for those of Guardian temperaments in church and in wider society suggests that church activities and services that appeal beyond the Guardian core are a particular priority. Acts of worship of that nature are probably not the cathedral carol service, where although we saw a small reduction from the church congregations in the number of Guardians among both men and women, it was only a fraction of the way towards the population norms. More likely are the various fresh expressions of church that have sprung up in the last few years. But alongside this, thought should be given to encouraging belonging through people, places and events as well as regular church activities.

Questions

- Might Psychological Type help explain the ways that I behave, especially when it comes to my church belonging?

- How much does it matter if some types are under- or over-represented in church congregations?

- Does Type give us any clues as to how to make churchgoing a better experience for men?

- Can, and should, Guardians be encouraged to run the church for the benefit of other temperaments?

Chapter 11

Models for motivation: exploring the world of Religious Orientation

Our last chapter used the concept of Psychological Type, which is very familiar in church circles. It allowed us to attach some numbers to the distinct populations that make up regular church worshippers, a cathedral carol service, clergy and the wider population. We were then able to make some useful observations and, I hope, provoke some thinking about how we can be more inclusive in the range of things that churches do. Numbers can be helpful. This next chapter takes us into a different set of numbers, and to another and somewhat less well-known area of theory. But I hope that the questions it raises will be as interesting and challenging.

Introducing Religious Orientation

The study of Religious Orientation, and in particular the attempts to measure it, have their foundations in the work of Gordon Allport in the USA. Studies from the 1940s onward consistently found that people belonging to and practising religions which teach tolerance and openness were nevertheless marked by positive associations between religion and prejudice. Was it simply a failure to properly understand what they were hearing in sermons and meant to believe and practise, or was there something else going on?

In an attempt to identify the particular factors at work, Allport and his colleague, Ross, set out to distinguish between two forms of Religious Orientation, Intrinsic and Extrinsic. Each was given a direct and accessible characterisation, a little like the characterisations we saw for different Psychological Types:

> Persons with this (Extrinsic) orientation are disposed to use religion for their own ends. The term is borrowed from axiology, to designate an interest that is held because it serves other, more ultimate interests. Extrinsic values are always instrumental and utilitarian. Persons with this orientation may find religion useful in a variety of ways—to provide security and solace, sociability and distraction, status and self-justification. The embraced creed is lightly held or else selectively shaped to fit more primary needs. In theological terms the extrinsic type turns to God, but without turning away from self.[10]

On the other hand:

> Persons with this (Intrinsic) orientation find their master motive in religion. Other needs, strong as they may be, are regarded as of less ultimate significance, and they are, so far as possible, brought into harmony with the religious beliefs and prescriptions. Having embraced a creed the individual endeavours to internalize it and follow it fully. It is in this sense that he lives his religion.[11]

If that still sounds a bit academic, it can be summed up in less complex language by saying that Extrinsic religiosity is motivated by something beyond itself. That's not necessarily a bad thing. External motivations can include my wish for assurance that I shall be reunited beyond this life with those whom I have loved and lost, or to be able to live without crippling guilt. By contrast, Intrinsic religiosity is its own reward.

At first read, that sounds as though we are dealing with two distinct types. In practice it has been found much more helpful to see both types of orientation as present in every person who has a religious motivation. Sets of questions have been developed that accord to each individual a score for two separate scales. What I and others have found in using them is that for somebody for whom their faith plays a very important role in their life, the scores for both scales will be high. Someone much less religious will come out lower on both.

The consensus of the research that followed over the next two decades established that prejudiced attitudes were associated with higher levels of Extrinsic orientation whilst higher levels of Intrinsic orientation were associated with lower prejudice in certain areas, most notably racism.

This theoretical model was expanded by a number of researchers, including Batson and Ventis, who in 1982 proposed that a third orientation, named as 'Quest', should also be considered. Once again, a direct and accessible characterisation was offered, and by now the language was a little more inclusive:

> An individual who approaches religion in this way recognises that he or she does not know, and probably never will know, the final truth about such matters. But still the questions are deemed important and however tentative and subject to change, answers are sought. There may not be a clear belief in a transcendent reality, but there is a transcendent, religious dimension to the individual's life.[12]

From these definitions of the three orientations, it is clear that what churches provide, both in terms of worship and more widely, may appeal to one type of orientation more than another. For example, it is now common across those parts of the Anglican Communion rooted in the catholic tradition, and in some places even for more evangelical churches, to hold special services at All Souls' Day which are directed towards those who have recently suffered bereavement. It is likely that such an occasion would be attended by many for whom religion is not a primary motivation, but who are seeking for reassurance and comfort in the face of death. This would be a classic example of Extrinsic religiosity. The appeal of the event is likely to be improved if this is understood by those planning and leading it, so that an appropriate balance can be found between affirming this type of religiosity and exposing those attending to the possibilities offered by the other orientations.

Again, different styles and content of preaching are also likely to appeal to the different orientations. A sermon that gives practical examples of how to live the Christian faith in everyday life should appeal to the Intrinsic orientation, but may have less to offer to the Quest orientation than would a sermon which posed questions for the congregation to explore, or which explained the different views held by Christians on some contentious matter, without branding one solution as correct. Extrinsic religiosity may be best supported by the sermon being engaging, well delivered and leaving the hearer with a good feeling.

Various scales to measure Religious Orientation have been produced over the years, and the measures have been used in a variety of ways. For the purposes of this book, I've adopted the New Indices of Religious Orientation.[13] The scales are each made up of nine questions, and depending on the answer given, a score from one to five is allocated. Adding up the scores to produce each index gives every participant three separate scores, each in the range nine to 45.

Although almost half of the cathedral carol service congregation were only occasional churchgoers, we've already seen that, for example, through figures for confirmation, very many of them have had a significant religious background, and that they take their faith seriously. So let's look at what was found when the Worcester carol service congregations completed the tests as part of the larger questionnaire I gave them.

Religious Orientation at the carol service

Age can often be an important factor in how people think and believe. So an obvious first question was to look at whether Religious Orientation appeared to change as people got older. For two out of the three indices—the Extrinsic and Quest scales—the answer was a fairly clear negative. In statistical studies a 'no' can be as important as a 'yes'. The lack of any change with age tells us that individuals are as likely to use their faith as a tool to achieve other goods (social standing, comfort in need) at any point in adult life. Again, it is not the case that younger people are more comfortable living with doubts than their elders; nor, by contrast, is there any greater recognition among older people that life is a journey where religious questions are often asked without final answers ever being received. It may of course be that both Extrinsic and Quest orientation are being driven by different factors at different ages, but to explore that would have required a very different study.

The picture was quite different when it came to the Intrinsic index. Older people scored much higher on this scale. My first response on discovering that was to wonder whether it might simply be that older people go to church more, and people who go to church score more highly on the Intrinsic scale. With a little bit more statistical analysis it was possible to take out the effect of more frequent churchgoing from the figures. And the answer remained the same. Perhaps what we are seeing is that older people have had time to allow their faith to impact more widely on their personal spirituality, religious practice and wider life.

I've mentioned that more religious people have been found to score more highly on all scales than those who are generally less religious. So we might expect some sort of link between the scores at the cathedral carol service and how often people go to church. As with age, there was no link with the scores on the Extrinsic scale. What I did find, along with a lesser but still significant positive association between churchgoing and Quest orientation, was a very strong link between Intrinsic orientation and frequency of church attendance. I did a bit more juggling with the number to see if this link remained even after allowing for the influence of age. It did. Perhaps to no surprise, where religion is strong in its impact on the whole of an individual's life, it is natural for that to be associated with regular participation in church worship.

There's a popular phrase among statisticians, that 'association is not causation'. The fact that people who go to church more times a year have a higher score of Intrinsic religious orientation doesn't tell whether it is churchgoing that makes faith lie more at the very centre of our lives, or if centring life around our faith makes us want to go to church more. My guess, for what it's worth, would be that this is a virtuous circle in which each reinforces the other. That suggests to me that as well as directly seeking to encourage people to come to church on more occasions, we are likely to grow congregations by working on other aspects of their religious life with those people who do not at present come often to church. Some of the examples in the chapter about engaging with occasional churchgoers on the *Five Marks of Mission* may be very relevant here. The person whose faith is deepened through participation in the food bank, the environmental clean-up, or the building project will be more likely to begin to want to attend worship more frequently.

Perhaps the finding that interested me most from these initial figures was the positive link between higher scores on the Quest scale and more frequent church attendance. My inclination would have been to expect the opposite; that it would be the occasional churchgoers who came with their questions and uncertainties, with a preparedness to acknowledge that they hadn't got the answers. Perhaps this is telling us an important fact about what a deep and mature Christian faith is like. I can recall, from my parish days, talking with people who came to join our church from other congregations. A repeated story was that they had come to faith and been nurtured within a fellowship that had provided very clear and certain answers to everything, from how they were to live their life to the way particular Bible passages had to be understood. For a while this had provided a secure environment in which to grow in faith; but only for a while. In time, they had found the certain answers less and less convincing and the clarity of the teaching constraining. They needed to be in a church where wrestling with questions was not a symptom of backsliding but a sign of serious engagement with God. They wanted a church where they would be helped and encouraged to enjoy their journey into faith, expecting their beliefs and attitudes to further change and develop.

There is a challenge here for churches of all types. For ones like my own, it raised questions of how we provided the safe and secure space in which people could come to faith, at a time when too much uncertainty might have left them feeling cut adrift. For churches with a more conservative outlook, the challenge is how to allow people to continue to deepen in faith at a point where they have to feel able to ask questions without having an answer imposed on them.

Is the carol congregation different?

In the last chapter we were able to look at some of the differences between people at the cathedral carol service and those attending as part of ordinary Sunday congregations in churches. Once again, thanks to some of my research colleagues, we have a comparison to look at. This time it's with studies also undertaken at cathedrals, but at the main Sunday morning services.

For the Quest scores, there was no discernible difference between Sunday and carol service churchgoers; both the average score and the spread of scores around that average, measured by what mathematicians call the 'standard deviation', were almost identical. For the Extrinsic scores, the carol service mean was noticeably lower, though the amount of spread around the mean was much the same. The biggest difference, though, came with the Intrinsic scores. For Sunday churchgoers, these averaged 32.7, but at the carol service the corresponding figure was only 27.5. Moreover, the spread of scores around the mean was much higher at the carol service, where the standard deviation was half as much again. Let's look now at what these differences in the scores of the two groups might mean.

It might have been thought that the cathedral carol service would show a higher Extrinsic average. There would be grounds for imagining some of its appeal would be to those who wish to assert or improve their social status (or at least their self-perception of it) by associating with the civic dignitaries, members of parliament and senior clerics who attend and read the lessons, or through association with the 'high culture' of the music offered on such occasions. But this isn't the case. The survey has found that people are actually less inclined to come to the carol service for reasons outside of religion than they are on a Sunday morning. That's an encouraging thing to know, and it corroborates what the occasional churchgoers among them had already told us about the spiritual dimensions to their attendance.

I've already remarked that Quest scores tend to be higher among both older people and those who go to church more often. With that in mind, I would have expected that the Quest average for the carol service would have been quite a bit lower than among people in a cathedral on a Sunday morning. The fact that it was almost identical to the Sunday mean provides a very strong indication that the carol service has a greater appeal to Quest orientation than a regular service does. Why might that be? I would look to the carol service emphasis on listening to the story in words and music, rather than having to respond to it through any creedal affirmation, or make the commitment implied by receiving Holy Communion. This is an act of Christian worship that, more than many others, is accessible to people who are willing to acknowledge and affirm their doubts and uncertainties and to see the spiritual life as a journey they have embarked upon, rather than a destination. It raises the question as to whether there are other ways in which churches can seek to broaden their appeal through special occasions to those occasional churchgoers who have as strong an element of Quest orientation in their lives as would normally be expected of somebody much more regular in their church attendance.

The combination of the lower Intrinsic mean and higher standard deviation for the carol service sample means that this population contains a high proportion of individuals with a much lower score on the Intrinsic orientation scale than almost any of those present on Sunday mornings. For example, a quarter of the congregation at the carol service had an Intrinsic score lower than all but about one in 50 of those who come to church on Sundays. However, there is much less difference at the upper ends of the scales.

Put together this tells us that the cathedral carol service has a much wider appeal across the range of Intrinsic religious orientation. It remains attractive to those with relatively high scores, yet its appeal to people who have comparatively low scores on the Intrinsic scale is one that is absent from cathedrals on a Sunday morning. Once again, this tells us that it is possible to devise an act of worship with an appeal that stretches much further than most regular services reach. And in doing so it presents us with a challenge to think about how services with similar appeal might be offered on a small number of occasions through the year.

Orientation and literal belief

In an earlier chapter we looked at the responses of people in the Harvest survey to a couple of questions about whether they believed literally that Jesus turned water into wine, and that God had created the world in six days and rested on the seventh. I've also shared a little bit of how the carol service congregation responded to questions that asked them whether they believed in certain aspects of the Christmas story, from the (non-biblical) donkey, via the shepherds and wise men to the virgin birth and on to the truth of Old Testament prophecies and the nature of the Christmas story as a theological whole. Furthermore, we've seen in both the previous chapter and the present one how researchers can build up numerical scales from the responses that people give to a range of independent but related statements. For somebody who enjoys playing with numbers as much as I do, that led to a very obvious question. Could I construct a scale that calculated how literally people believe in the Christmas story, and would that scale be strong enough to be put alongside other things we know about them? To my delight, what I constructed passed all the standard tests of statistical reliability. We could now compare literal belief in Christmas with other elements of the carol service survey.

The first thing of note was that the new scale for literal Christmas beliefs showed that men and women were equally likely to hold such views. Older people were seen to be more inclined to literal belief, but there was an even stronger correlation with church attendance. The latter is particularly unsurprising as it would be expected that regular churchgoing would be associated with stronger levels of Christian belief in general, and that some of this would be reflected in a higher level of literal belief. A little careful statistical work made it clear that the higher level of literal beliefs among older people was entirely accounted for by the fact that they go to church more often. Older people are no more literal in their understanding of the Christmas story than are younger ones who go to church as frequently.

The thrust of this chapter, though, is about the concept and use of Religious Orientation and the three indices that constitute it. So how does literal belief relate to each of them?

Firstly, after taking account of age, sex and churchgoing frequency, and the other orientations, higher levels of Intrinsic Religious Orientation came out as a very strong predictor for more literal beliefs about the Christmas story. All this is notwithstanding the fact that the statements used to derive the scale have no inbuilt bias in them that should produce literal interpretations of Christmas as a consequence. This result falls neatly into line with previous research that has discovered a relationship between Intrinsic orientation and various aspects of what might be described as religious conservatism.

The results for Extrinsic orientation largely replicate the picture, but with lower levels of positive association with literal Christmas beliefs. Yet here again there is nothing in the questions used to build the Extrinsic scale that forces towards such beliefs. The picture isn't quite the same as for Intrinsic orientation, though, because earlier studies have found no corresponding direct link between Extrinsic religiosity and religious conservatism. What we now know is that there is a small but significant positive association between Extrinsic orientation and literal views about Christmas.

The findings with regard to the Quest index present a very different picture. Once the impact of all the other factors has been taken out, what is left is a clear predictive element in the reverse direction: higher Quest scores are associated with lower levels of literal belief in the Christmas story. Once again, there is no reason to assume from the questions used in compiling the index that Quest orientation is antithetical to literal beliefs; rather, that they would be likely to be held more provisionally. Indeed, earlier research has not suggested that Quest orientation on its own is a predictor, one way or the other, of traditional views. What has now been discovered is that when all other factors have been controlled for, Quest orientation does in fact have a clear negative link with holding literal beliefs about Christmas.

Having established the relationships between literal Christmas belief and Religious Orientation, let's now reflect on what this means for ministry and mission.

What we've found through the link between Intrinsic religiosity and literal Christmas views suggests that if the promotion of Intrinsic orientation is seen as a mission goal, then an approach that goes along with or encourages innate literalism may produce the best results. This would be particularly so if the position of the church is that Extrinsic and Quest orientations are not to be encouraged on wider grounds of churchmanship, teaching or tradition. Equally, a church that promotes only those aspects of Christian life that are associated with Intrinsic religiosity, and discourages other orientations, is likely both to attract and sustain more conservative Christians and to find existing members becoming more literal in their beliefs. We might add that where the mission of the church is defined in terms of sustaining and working with the dominant Intrinsic orientation, then liturgies and preaching that take their starting point from biblical criticism are likely to be less successful.

Looking elsewhere, parishes and churches of a liberal outlook should not be afraid that the traditional elements of the service of Nine Lessons and Carols are out of keeping with their standpoint. The evidence of the present study is that these services appeal to the Quest orientation that has been found, once other factors are controlled for, to be associated with less literal views. Moreover, 'Quest-friendly' approaches have particular value in these places. It can be seen that mission strategies which encourage Quest orientation rather than Intrinsic or Extrinsic are the ones most likely to appeal to those of less literal Christmas beliefs and hence probably less conservative religious positions more generally. Conversely, where a Quest-friendly approach is adopted, perhaps in order to work with younger, more occasional churchgoers, it is likely to reduce levels of conservatism in the congregation.

Irrespective of churchmanship traditions, Christmas remains a unique phenomenon across denominations and around the globe. Very large numbers of occasional churchgoers turn up to services such as Midnight Mass, Christingle and the carol service. The cathedral service of Nine Lessons and Carols is a good example, but far from alone. We've seen that it has a clearly stronger appeal not only to younger people and less frequent churchgoers, but to those for whom Quest plays a more prominent role than Intrinsic, when compared with the regular Sunday morning churchgoers. We've also discovered that such people are less literal in their views about the Christmas story and hence arguably less traditional in their religious views more generally. In terms of the mission priorities of the church at large and the cathedral in particular, these results show a strong case for meeting these 'Questers' on their own territory and presenting them with expressions of Christian faith that are congruent with their relatively liberal beliefs not only at Christmas but on other occasions too.

More generally, all churches that wish to reach out to the religious needs and aspirations of their parishioners who only come from time to time should be wary of changing the format of their carol service into something that makes higher doctrinal demands or that downplays the element of searching and provisionality in faith.

Questions

- Can I think of aspects of my own faith that fit each of the three dimensions of Religious Orientation?

- Do I see myself as mostly of one particular orientation?

- Are there things my church could do differently to encourage those whose orientation is different from the majority?

- What might effective mission to each of the three dimensions of Religious Orientation look like in my church?

Chapter 12

Never on Sunday: the opportunities and challenges of Sunday worship

As with each of the two previous sections of this book, I want to conclude the present one with a short worked example. Although the material about Psychological Type and Religious Orientation was gathered at what we have called throughout this book an 'event', it has implications for the way in which worship is constructed and delivered, and how churches handle changes to that pattern, at regular Sunday services. It is Sunday worship that remains the visible 'shop window' of the church. If we are to embody a wider vision of Christian belonging, we need to do at least some of that here.

The challenge of change

A few years ago, I was speaking with a vicar whose church was located close by a popular waterway, well used by the narrowboats that provide both a temporary home to holidaymakers and a permanent one to a distinct section of Britain's traveller community. The priest had come up with a brainwave, to provide a handful of moorings close by the church, and to publicise that these were available for any who wanted to tie up their boat for a short while and join the congregation for worship. The church council took a very different line, summed up by one member stating, 'We don't want that sort of person here.' It's a phrase which is not very often put so bluntly, but which provides the boundaries for the outreach that many churches are prepared to undertake.

For such a church, were an honest mission statement to be written, it would probably look something like this:

> St Nemo's is a friendly and welcoming church. We wish to grow by doing the things we like best, and doing them as well as we possibly can. We believe that this will encourage those others in our parish who like the same things as we do, to join us. We particularly welcome those who are younger than ourselves. We will encourage them to take over responsibility for keeping things the way we like them, in preparation for the time when we no longer have the strength, energy and money to do so.

When I have been involved in working with a parish towards the recruitment of a new priest, it has been quite common to be presented with a profile of the next vicar that has been full of phrases about the church needing to find fresh vision, and looking for somebody to lead them into a time of change. Come the day itself, after the final candidate has gone and a decision has to be made, it hasn't always been easy to hold the local representatives to what they have asked for, in the teeth of a wish that they would like the 'safest' candidate. It's a natural human reaction; change in theory is less scary than change in practice. And those charged with representing their parish in the selection of a new vicar know that they will be ones who are called to account by their congregation if their choice ruffles feathers. The bishop, archdeacon and patron will be elsewhere, handling their next vacancy. It's summed up in the popular cartoon of a church committee, the leader of whom is saying:

> OK, so we've agreed the profile for our next pastor. We're looking for a dynamic, visionary and energetic man or woman of God, under whose leadership things will stay exactly as they always have been.

Lest this be thought of as mere caricature, an experienced seminary staff member in the USA, who had spent many years preparing people for church ministry, and seeking to encourage them to be missionary in their outlook, recently carried out research among a large number of members of congregations to check that what he thought he was preparing new pastors for was what those receiving them wanted. When he analysed the data that came back, there was a very clear winner. What churchgoers most wanted was 'somebody who will look after me and my family'.

So I don't underestimate the challenge involved in calling churches to broaden their outlook. If it works, it will almost inevitably involve things being done in ways that make many of the original congregation feel less comfortable. What's more, as I discovered in my own parish ministry, there will come a moment when some of those who have been attracted by the new developments will graduate to positions of leadership and responsibility within the church. They will want to cease to be the guests who gratefully accept what is being offered to them, even if it has been cooked with some awareness of their dietary needs. Rather, they will wish to take up the role of hosts; to become the ones who plan and prepare the menu. At least to some extent, the price for the enhancement of their sense of belonging will be paid by those of us who might feel we belong a little less.

Imperfect belonging

The two previous chapters cover the areas where perhaps the challenge of changing to include others will be felt at its clearest in public worship. Sermons that always provide clear and authoritative answers to life's questions, something that might appeal strongly to a person with a low level of Quest Religious Orientation, will be positively off-putting to a person who needs to be allowed to explore the mystery of God, and to discover provisional truths that are constantly subject to challenge and revision along the way. Services where the Giving of the Peace and the singing of emotionally laden songs account for far more time than the Bible readings and preaching may offer little to an individual who prefers to engage with the world through Thinking rather than Feeling. In those chapters I offered some encouragement for churches to find suitable special occasions throughout the year, where a service of a very different style, and hence perhaps a different appeal, could be held. Both carol services and Harvest Festivals appeared to be doing that to a degree. But to conclude that this broader appeal can only take place outside of the regular parish services is to concede too much too soon.

Are we actually, with regard to Sunday worship, in what mathematicians refer to as a 'zero sum game'? Is it the case that every passionate praise song that draws me closer to God is alienating the person sat by me? If so, then our missionary strategy perhaps should simply be to see that the range of churches in an area covers the widest possible variety of distinct styles, and encourage everybody to find the one that suits them best. To some extent, of course, that is exactly what already happens. Different denominations, and different churches within the same denomination, have their distinctive ethos and style. In an area of widespread access to transport, those of us who are mobile will go wherever suits us best. If a particular style proves less generally popular, then that church will decline or die. In some cases, it will be handed over and planted back into by a congregation with a different and more successful ethos, and then grow again. There may be places where this is the right strategy to follow.

Yet I feel constantly drawn back to a wider vision, one that underpins the notion of a parish church that seeks to engage with a wide sector of its local community, to know and be known by those who live within it, not simply to be the group who come from afar to occupy a particular building once or twice a week. And this poses the question as to how much of what goes on in church, especially during public worship, has to fit with my own natural (and I'd want by this stage of the book to call them 'God-given') preferences? Does everything need to be just the way I would choose it? If not 100 per cent, then do I require a clear majority to suit me? Or can I belong in a church where my personality and Religious Orientation are a minority, but a minority that is accepted and cherished, with just enough of what I like best?

We can take the sermon as an example. On occasion I've made a deliberate effort in my preaching to offer something that appeals to the emotions and something that appeals to logic. I've incorporated sections that engage our senses and others that express the use of intuition. I offer a mixture of answers and questions. I often try to leave people with some task to perform or issue to think through over the following week. My personal experience is that few people remember a whole sermon for very long. I certainly don't. What they may do is catch hold of something, a phrase or image that particularly attracts or challenges them, and retain it for reflection or action. It's an old adage that mostly preachers are preaching to themselves, but it's a false one. The challenge of preaching is to offer something to the people who share our faith, but otherwise are not like ourselves at all.

In the same way, I suspect that church intercessions could be structured to increase the number of those who are genuinely being drawn close to God through them. Thoughts and feelings on the issues of the day can be offered and people held before him for healing and restoration. Images from the senses can be interspersed with invocations of mystery. Specific requests can be combined with appeals for new insight and greater wisdom.

In churches that follow the set Bible readings for the day, there will often be a balance of styles from poetry and story to law and prophecy; from argument and action to pleading and praise. It's harder to use scripture in ways that broaden its appeal and impact in places that focus on a single reading, especially if a sermon series means that for several weeks or longer, attention is being paid to just one book.

Music remains especially difficult to get right. Partly because, except at services like the cathedral carols, we are expected to actively join in with every hymn and song. By contrast, we can pick from the scriptures, sermon and prayers the things that strike us, and let much of the rest pass gently by. I have stood before congregations and noticed somebody quite obviously not joining in with a particular hymn. Usually they look very stony-faced and I suspect that they are feeling only marginally less uncomfortable than if they had remained seated. I can empathise; there are certain hymns and songs that I really don't like having to sing, and even some where I automatically miss out or change a word or line. My suspicion is that the negative impact of singing a hymn that jars with our personality or position is rather stronger than the positive impact when we sing one that just hits the spot. Perhaps in larger churches we should have more songs that are simply sung to us by a choir or music group, whilst in smaller churches, where musical quality can be an issue, we should from time to time listen to a recorded piece, whilst silently following the printed words.

Multiple belonging

If my church is not providing all that is needed for my particular personality and Type, are there other times and places where my remaining needs can be met, whilst enabling me not just to hang in but to enjoy being a part of a church where I am in a minority?

There were times for me, even as a vicar, when the dominant style of worship in the local church was not what I would have chosen. There was, however, enough in it that did sustain me, so that I found myself quite able to worship in it. I was even able to lead it sufficiently well for the congregation to grow. But something was missing for me, and that something was met through my membership of the Franciscan family. On a regular basis I was part of a different group, where the worship fed me what I was otherwise missing. And crucially I was there not just as a guest, as though I had popped into the church in the next-door parish for a 'top up'. I was there as somebody who truly belonged.

Being part of the Third Order of the Society of St Francis continues to give me a great deal. It provides me with a group of fellow Christians with whom I have developed a strong sense of belonging. When I moved, firstly from South Yorkshire to the West Midlands, then later from there to take up my current post, on each occasion I have found a group, meeting regularly, and ready to receive and befriend me. This has continued to give me a sense of belonging with St Francis himself.

When I read the stories of his life, tell them to others, or discuss them in a small group, talking about Francis is very much like speaking of a good friend. The Franciscan family has also given me special places with which to belong. Memories of Assisi, although I have not been able to go there for many years, remain vivid and sustaining. In this country several of the houses occupied by the First Order Franciscan brothers and sisters have become precious to me. And, of course, I attend from time to time at large special gatherings. I belong through all four dimensions of the model we have been exploring.

The Franciscan order could never have become my principle church. It doesn't gather often enough and it doesn't have the necessary locus for engagement within the local community. Wisely, nobody can be admitted as a Franciscan Tertiary who is not part of, and committed to, a local church. But what my experience of being part of it has shown me is that I can belong to more than one expression of Christian life, and that this plurality of membership does not pull me in different directions; rather, each supports the other. What Franciscan belonging has done for me is something that I am finding is increasingly being offered, through a wide range of emerging gatherings and communities, to many others. Having a particular home in these groups sustains us for belonging in churches where otherwise not enough of what is on offer will meet our need and preferences.

Having extolled the virtues of multiple belonging, through organisations and communities that redress the missing elements of local church life, I need to end with a short warning to those communities, especially at a time when new ones are coming in to being and others are experiencing significant growth. The temptation can be for the community to seek to become the church itself. A sign of that happening is usually that the organisation seeks to accrete to itself more and more of the facets of church life. As it does so, it creates an infrastructure that requires servicing, and draws some of its most committed members into fulfilling those roles. The level of activity increases further and soon passes a vital point. At this stage the members are no longer being empowered and energised to belong to their local churches; instead they are being drawn away from them. In particular, those withdrawing from church life in order to devote more to the community will often be among the most gifted, willing and experienced church members. When this happens repeatedly, the community loses the confidence of local churches, clergy especially, and is seen not as a support but a rival. Communities that are primarily set up to complement church membership need to hold firm to that vision and resist the temptation to become more than they have been called to be.

Questions

- Has this book helped me to identify where my church is being resistant to change? What might we do about it?

- Can I recall a sermon that has tried to offer different things to different people? Has it worked for me?

- Are there Christian organisations and groups outside of my local church that help sustain me for belonging?

- Are there groups that would tend to draw me away from my commitment to my local church?

Concluding remarks

I began this book by quoting the words of William Temple, that the Christian Church is unique in being an institution existing primarily for the benefit of those who are not its members. It was the Church in its organised, institutional form to which he was referring, not the Church as the total aggregate of all those who, to some extent or other, believe in and seek to follow Jesus Christ; those who are, in biblical language, members of his Body. What I've tried to offer in the chapters which followed that introduction is an understanding of the difference between the two, in order that the mission to which those of us who are part of the organised life of the Church are called can be properly undertaken, with the cooperation of, and for the good of, those who Temple reminded us are its true beneficiaries. Both the chapters that have developed and tested the theory and those that have served as our 'worked examples' have made clear that being informed and aware of the invisible factors at play within our individual differences does not of itself provide easy solutions towards building a more inclusive Church.

Nevertheless, even the most daunting journey is made up of individual steps. Throughout the book I have sought to offer hints and ideas of things that churches can try out; ways of encouraging people to belong more deeply, whether or not that deeper belonging results in more frequently attending church services. In particular, I've tried to offer a model for mission that embraces the various fresh expressions of church that have successfully increased activity membership in many places, and yet extends it to people, places and events. Most important of all, I hope I may have convinced you that mission is not just something that a committed core does to others, but a task in which all those who belong, by whatever mode their belonging is most effected, can join in.

If this book helps some of you to become part of such a mission, it will have done its job.

Bibliography

The ideas explored in this book were first developed through a series of academic papers and chapters published between 2004 and 2012.

Walker, D.S., 'Private property and public good.' In J. Martineau, L.J. Francis and P. Francis (eds), *Changing Rural Life: A Christian Response to Key Rural Issues* (Canterbury Press, 2004), pp. 79–98.

Walker, D.S., 'Belonging to rural church and society: Theological and religious perspectives', *Rural Theology*, 4.2, 85–97, 2008.

Walker, D.S., 'Communion by extension: discrepancies between policy and practice', *Rural Theology*, 6.1, 11–25, 2008.

Walker, D.S., 'The social significance of Harvest Festivals in the countryside: An empirical enquiry among those who attend', *Rural Theology*, 7.1, 3–16, 2009.

Walker, D.S., 'The religious beliefs and attitudes of rural Anglican churchgoers: Weekly and occasional attendees', *Rural Theology*, 8.2, 159–72, 2010.

Walker, D.S., 'Marks of Mission and ways of belonging: Shaping the Anglican agenda for occasional churchgoers in the countryside', *Journal of Anglican Studies*, 9.1, 100–116, 2010.

Walker, D.S., L.J. Francis and M. Robbins, 'You don't have to go to church to be a good Christian: The implicit religion of rural Anglican churchgoers celebrating harvest', *Implicit Religion*, 13.3, 319–25, 2010.

Walker, D.S., 'Personal prayer, church attendance and social capital among rural churchgoers: Quantitative empirical methods as a tool for mission and ministry', *Rural Theology*, 9.1, 39–47, 2011.

Walker, D.S., 'O come all ye thinking types: The wider appeal of the cathedral carol service', *Mental Health, Religion & Culture*, 15.1, 987–95, 2012.

Walker, D.S., 'Measuring the New Indices of Religious Orientation at the cathedral carol service: Internal consistency and reliability among a distinctively wide ranging sample', *Journal of Beliefs and Values*, 33.1, 117–22, 2012.

Walker, D.S., 'Attending the Service of Nine Lessons and Carols at a rural cathedral: An empirical study in religious orientation and motivational style', *Rural Theology*, 10.1, 56–69, 2012.

Notes

1 G. Davie, *Religion in Britain since 1945: Believing without belonging* (Blackwell, 1994).

2 R. Thomas, *Counting People In* (SPCK, 2003), p. 7.

3 W. Brueggemann, *The Land* (Fortress Press, 2002), p. xi.

4 Archbishops' Council, *Mission-shaped Church* (Church House Publishing, 2004).

5 Archbishops' Council, *Public Worship with Communion by Extension* (Church House Publishing, 2001), p. 32.

6 Anglican Communion Office, *Five Marks of Mission*, www. anglicancommunion.org/ministry/mission/fivemarks.cfm.

7 L.J. Francis, *Faith and Psychology* (Darton, Longman & Todd, 2005).

8 L.J. Francis, M. Robbins and C. Craig, 'The psychological type profile of Anglican churchgoers in England', *International Journal of Practical Theology* (2011), p. 244.

9 Francis, Robbins and Craig, 'The psychological type profile of Anglican churchgoers', p. 244.

10 G.W. Allport and J.M. Ross, 'Personal Religious Orientation and Prejudice', *Journal of Personality and Social Psychology* (1967), p. 434.

11 Allport and Ross, 'Personal Religious Orientation and Prejudice', p. 434.

12 C.D. Batson and W.L. Ventis, *The Religious Experience: A Social-Psychological Perspective* (Oxford University Press, 1982), p. 150.

13 L.J. Francis, 'Exploring the New Indices of Religious Orientation (NIRO): Conceptualisation and measurement', *Mental Health, Religion and Culture* (2007), pp. 585–602.